Praise for

THE NIGHT I GOT DAVID BOWIE LAID *sorta*

The Intimate and Antic Accounts of an Original Gangster

"Edwin Heaven's excellent 'kiss and tell-all' has all the makings of a runaway bestseller! I give it FIVE cherry bombs!"

— CHERIE CURRIE

Voice of The Runaways, author of *Neon Angel*, actress, chainsaw artist

"Strap it down and strap in, folks! Edwin Heaven is coming in hotter than hell with his new memoir, and you definitely don't want to miss it. Salacious, shocking, titillating and hilarious – everything you could possibly want – and I urge you to come along for the ride. I did, and I'm still dizzy!"

— SALLY MANN ROMANO

Author of *The Band's With Me: Tour 1964-1975*

"WOW! Edwin Heaven spills enough tea to float the Queen Mary! This page-turner tells all not just about Rock Royalty such as Bowie, Mick, Jimi, Iggy, Dee Dee, and James Brown, but also Hollywood Heavyweights like Steve McQueen, Jack Nicholson, Francis Coppola, Robin Williams, and Kim Novak. Read this and you'll learn enough stories to be the center of attention at cocktail parties! It's like pop-culture history retold by Ken Russell!"

— LAURA ALBERT a.k.a. JT LEROY

Author of *Sarah, The Heart Is Deceitful Above All Things* and *Harold's End*

"Everyone knows Edwin Heaven writes like hell, but we have been waiting all these unconscionable years for him to drag out his steamer trunk of stories. Worth it. Edwin spins his tales with wit, whimsy and a delightful soupcon of depravity that gives the whole thing its spice. Long live Edwin Heaven. I eagerly await Volume Two."

— JOEL SELVIN

Author of *Hollywood Eden* and *Here Comes The Night*, and music critic

"Edwin Heaven is one of the most original, clever and witty writers in America today, and *The Night I Got David Bowie Laid (Sorta)* is his masterpiece. This slice of San Francisco rock in the 1970s is served up like a delicious piece of cherry pie and a scoop of ice cream – tasty, filling, not necessarily good for you, but it sure does go down good."

— MARSHALL TERRILL

Steve McQueen: The Life and Legend of a Hollywood Icon and *Elvis and the Colonel*

"Edwin Heaven has written a rock and roll memoir for the ages. His encounters with the greats make for a terrific read, but best of all is Heaven's comic, exuberant self at the center of it."

— ELIZABETH MCKENZIE

Author of *The Dog of the North, Stop That Girl, The Portable Veblen*

THE

NIGHT

I GOT

DAVID

BOWIE

LAID

sorta

by

EDWIN

HEAVEN

Disclaimer

This work of autobiographical short stories, titled *The Night I Got David Bowie Laid sorta* depicts actual events in the life of the author, and is told as truthfully as recollection permits. The names of some individuals have been changed to ensure their reputations suffer no harm. The content within this book is provided for information and entertainment purposes only, and, as such, may be subject to memory, interpretation, and personal bias. The author disclaims any liability for any consequences, misunderstandings, or disputes that may arise as a result of the content in this memoir. By reading this book, you acknowledge that you have read and understood the disclaimer and that you will use the content responsibly and at your own discretion.

Book design by Gabriela Rivas
Cover art by Prairie Prince

Cover photos by:

Andrew Kent (David Bowie)
Robert Altman (Iggy Pop)
Gerald Kudo (Re Styles)
Art Taylor (Edwin Heaven)

Printed in the United States of America

FIRST EDITION

"Lazy"
Words and Music by Jennifer Anderson
Copyright© 1977
All rights reserved. Used by permission.

"Suicide Child"
Words and Music by Alejandro Escovedo and Jeffrey Olener
Copyright© 1977
All rights reserved. Used by permission

LIBRARY OF CONGRSS
CATALOGING-IN-PUBLICATION DATA

ISBN 979-8-218-41621-8

Heaven, Edwin
The night i got david bowie laid (sorta), nonfiction/ Edwin Heaven

www.edwinheaven.com

WARNING:

This book contains copious amounts of
sex, drugs and rock 'n roll.

This one's for my daughter, Audrey,
and Artie, the grandfather she never met.

Art's last letter

"Sometimes you will never know the value of something,
until it becomes a memory."

~ Theo Geisel (a.k.a. Dr. Seuss)

"I have a memory like an elephant.
I remember every elephant I ever met."

~ Herb Caen, author and Pulitzer Prize-winning columnist

CONTENTS

AN AUTHOR'S NOTE

Memory is nonlinear (for me, at least) which might explain why this memoir doesn't begin at the beginning or end at the end and starts somewhere near the middle.

Like *Pulp Fiction*. (Or, in this case, Pulp Nonfiction.)

It's how time rolls—backflips, leapfrogs, pogos, sways and does the wah-watusi.

That said, I had a ball writing it. An eight ball. (He said, in jest.)

The author being funky wearing a Tubes shirt of himself.

Art: Prairie Prince
Photo: Jonathan Postal

1977
THE NIGHT I GOT
DAVID BOWIE LAID *sorta*

— BERLIN —

We were coked out of our skulls. Thick white lines laid out for the "Thin White Duke." Our nostrils kept in step with the Bolivian marching powder.

Left-right-left. Left-right-left.

The room was closed-off from the rest of the party, windowless and smoke-filled. The thin man chain-smoked—Gitanes, no less—would light the next one with the last one, each time lighting one for me. (A debt of gratitude is owed. For after that night, I would give up smoking for good.)

His bodyguard—muscled arms folded like Mr. Clean—stood watch at the door. Every so often he'd step aside to usher in some guests. In particular, those who were holding.

His Grace will see you now. And so will his sniffer.

Artists and punks, bikers and babes, wheelers and dealers. The latter, especially. Typically, after a minute or two of doting, out came the dope. A toot-toot here, a toot-toot there, everywhere a toot-toot. Then tootle-oo, off they'd scoot to make room for the next snoot full.

I guess you could say, when on Mars do as the Spiders do.

I left some hours later, but not before introducing him to a hot little number.

Her name: Berlin.

— A STREETWALKING CHEETAH —

Earlier that evening, the message light on my answering machine was blinking as if it had a tic disorder. The remedy was simple. I pushed Play.

"Edwin," said the easygoing baritone, "David's at the Mabuhay. Get your punk-ass down there."

Beep.

It was a familiar voice. I hit Rewind. Yes, just as I thought: it was the voice of a streetwalking cheetah. So, the likelihood that the David mentioned was the one and same David who had recently toured with him. So, duh! No need to put a ray gun to my head. Quicker than you could say *freak out in a moonage daydream*, my punk-ass was down there.

* * *

EDWIN HEAVEN

— THE FAB MAB —

What CBGB was to punk in NYC, the Mabuhay was in SF. It was located on Broadway, a street known for its strip joints and adult theaters—and now ripped jeans and sinsemilla joints, as well as the arbitrary spiked hair and safety pins. On the Mab's façade was a two-story tall mural of the Nuns, the f rst punk band to play there. A band, incidentally, that I was managing.

Suddenly I heard what sounded like a three-car collision. I looked up and down the street, but there were no mangled cars.

The racket was coming from inside the club, where, in the mosh pit, white punks in sweat-soaked tees shoved and slammed. Some tossed wicker baskets of stale popcorn speckled with rat droppings. Clubbers rarely *ate* the complimentary popcorn. And, evidently,

25

Photo: Craig Simpson © Edwin Heaven

neither did the rats. The jarring band onstage didn't mind being pelted with popcorn. In all probability, it was taken as a compliment.

I spotted toward the back of the room a large, broad-shouldered man I had pegged as the bodyguard and over one of his broad shoulders there emerged a shock of flame-hair, a pale angular face and the world's most iconic mismatched-eyes.

I ploughed through the crowd and when I got there the bodyguard gave me one of those searching looks as if I might be brandishing a stiletto or a curdled blintz. It was his job, I suppose, to always think the worst. Then deciding I was probably the most innocuous person in the club, he stepped aside.

"Hello, David," I said. "I'm Edwin Heaven. Jimmy's friend."

Jimmy, of course, being James Osterberg, Jr. a.k.a. Streetwalking Cheetah a.k.a. The Idiot a.k.a. Iggy Pop.

David flashed a charming snaggletooth smile. "Where's the party, Edwin?"

"David," I said, "*you're* the party."

* * *

EDWIN HEAVEN

— GRUMPY —

So, there we were. David Effing Bowie and moi, bobbing our heads to some two-chord nonsense.

Five years earlier, I was walking my Afghans in Sausalito when a gorgeous redhead stopped me on the street. "Googy!" she squealed, signaling that she was from Philly. She was carrying an LP. "You gotta hear this," she said, "it's freaking fantastic!" And so, of course, I brought her up to my apartment. That night she introduced me to *Hunky Dory*. She also introduced me to her spectacular breasts and everything else south of her neckline, and, needless to say, I've been a big Bowie fan ever since.

At the time, I was managing a power trio—along the lines of a Blue Cheer or a Jimi Hendrix Experience—that I named Sperm

Whale. Like I would do years later for the Nuns, I plastered slick posters all around the Bay Area—on telephone poles and store fronts, head shops and record stores, in display windows of boutiques, on just about everything short of sandwich boards—proclaiming "SPERM WHALE IS COMING." But what actually created the buzz wasn't simply a grassroots saturation campaign but the poster's image of an attractive young woman of ample proportions wearing nothing but a tiny black heart on a portly cheek. (Not *that* cheek.)

Believe me when I say it was no cakewalk finding such a model. I approached just about every zaftig woman I saw and asked if she'd be interested in posing nude. I was snarled at, laughed at, even got slapped once, and, on one occasion, got bit by a spider monkey wearing a miniature bellhop's hat—the pet of legendary restaurateur Juanita Musson who was fond of wearing XXXL muumuus. I figured one heavyset woman would know others. A chub club of sorts. Juanita was a kind and generous woman and poured gin over the wound, then poured me a double. That week, plus-size women came to my apartment in droves, stripped down to their panties (or, in one instance, her boxer shorts), but not one of them quite fit the bill. Either they were round enough but not pretty enough, or they were pretty enough but not round enough.

I might never have found the right model if not for the Mitchell brothers, Jim and Artie (whose porn classic *Behind the Green Door* not only graced the genre with higher production values, but also introduced Marilyn Chambers, the all-American blonde pictured on every box of Ivory Snow). Jan Harmon was a cute, roly-poly "adult entertainer." She and her hubby, a gaunt little man who resembled the great underground cartoonist Robert Crumb, would also perform various sexual acts, live and in person, for small private parties. Photographer Mikel Covey cleverly used a fisheye lens to give her an even more circular appearance. The ultra wide-angle lens also gave the impression that the three handsome, bare-chested musicians, with wavy hair down to their shoulders, were peering out from behind Jan, their heads appearing to be half the size of her breasts. It would become *Rolling Stone's* "Poster of the Year."

But great posters, alone, do not great bands make and on the morning, following their highly touted debut at the Kabuki Theater, a prickly newspaperman (perhaps especially peeved because he had been kept up way past his bedtime) wrote, with great impertinence: "Hype Can't Help Sperm Whale."

But what does all this have to do with David Bowie?

This unflattering review also included a callous remark that implied how little I knew about music when I said, "David Bowie is going to be the biggest thing since the Beatles."

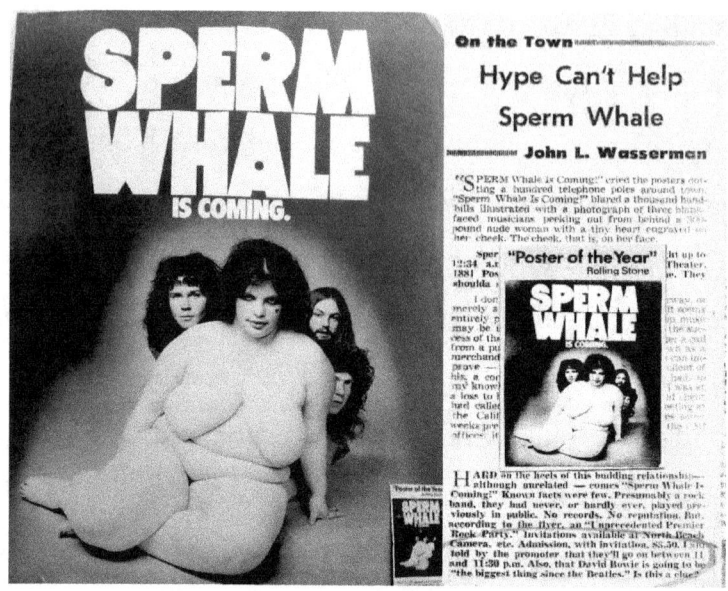

Photo: Mikel Covey © Edwin Heaven

Now, mind you, this was back in 1972 and my opinion had been based solely upon the *Hunky Dory* album. About a month after this nasty review, out comes *The Rise and Fall of Ziggy Stardust and the Spiders from Mars* album, and it would rise to the tippy top of the *Billboard* charts, making Bowie a rock star of the highest magnitude, and giving me, most definitely, the proverbial last laugh.

And so, when the 4/4 pounding finally stopped, I turned to David and said, "Me thinks it's time to fucking party. What say you?"

"I say," he said, "fucking parties are my favorite kind."

I laughed. "Okay, hang tight, gonna make a call. Be back in a jiff."

"A whiff?"

"Yeah, David," I said, taking the hint. "That, too."

I made my way across the clammy crush, dodging a thrashing arm and splattering beer to the office of Dirk Dirksen, located not surprisingly near the box office's cash register.

The door was closed, so I knocked. From the other side came a voice not unlike Barney Fife pretending to be badass. "If you're not a Brink's armored guard," it said, "or Rock Hudson, go away!"

I was neither, but entered just the same. "Ha! You wish you needed an armored truck!"

He was reared back in his chair, stocking-feet on top the desk, a sweet-tempered black Schnoodle on his lap. "You're certainly no Rock Hudson, that's for sure," he said in his usual tetchy manner.

"And you're no Doris Day."

On the desk, along with his feet, were stacks of cash. Calling them stacks is being magnanimous. They were about as tall as a short stack at IHOP, more than likely comprised mostly of singles. The night's take couldn't have been more than five hundred considering there was no real headliner and, being a weeknight, admission was a scant three bucks. Would cost three times as much to get in on a weekend. Tonight, after the bands got their split, they would be lucky to pocket thirty bucks apiece. But, by and large, the bands didn't give a shit. They were either blitzed, stoned, or coked out of their simple minds. Mostly, they just wanted to play in front of a manic crowd. See their name on a flyer. Hang out. Or get a slice of hair-pie after the show. The Nuns would be headlining in a couple more days, and they always packed 'em in. They could pack the club ten nights in a row and, at the time, were the moneymakers that kept the Mabuhay going.

"You'll probably need an armored truck Friday," I said. "Maybe two."

Dirk feigned annoyance, but didn't dispute. If he were one of the Seven Dwarfs, he'd be Grumpy. That's if Grumpy had a mustache, wore aviator-shaped glasses and, occasionally, a rubber penis on his nose.

"I take it you know who's out there tonight," I said.

"Yes, and if I'd known beforehand," he said, frowning at a skimpy stack of dollars, "would've slipped his name on the marquee."

Dirk had a reputation for being a nasty, cantankerous curmudgeon. He'd insult the customers. Call them cretins, maggots, insects, animals and morons. Yet the crowd ate it up.

Once, when I was directing a low budget flick and needed a gun as a prop, I asked Dirk if he had one. "Yeah," he said, "come on over." So, I raced across town expecting to borrow a Luger or a Mauser, but, as it turned out, it was a little starter pistol. Perfect for track and field, maybe, but not for film noir. Fortunately, in a detective's shoulder holster it didn't look quite as puny. My point being, Dirk would come off like a jackass or an asshole, but it was all just an act. He was, at heart, a performance artist and the Mabuhay was his stage. And, in truth, if you didn't know him personally, you'd think he was a big ol' badass pit bull. But, in actuality, he was a sweet little cuddly mutt. In other words, with Dirk, you're expecting a bazooka and, instead, get a cap pistol.

"So, what is it you want?" he said, feet propped up, dog on lap. "You can see I'm busy."

Yeah, rrright. "I won't be but a minute," I said. "Just need to make a quick call."

"Well, if I find out it's long-distance, gonna deduct it from the Nuns' door."

"If not for the Nuns, would you even have a door?"

He made a face. "Dummy!" he said.

I was taken aback. "Me?"

"Not you. *Him.* Dummy's his name." He held his dog at arm's length with one hand while fanning the air with the other. "Pew, Dummy, pew! No more kielbasa for you!"

I gave the dog a gentle pat. "Don't take it too personal," I told him. "Your daddy calls everyone he likes dummy."

With a nimble stocking-foot, Dirk slid the phone across the desk.

With the tip of my thumb and forefinger, I picked up the handset like it was a soiled sock. "Hope I don't get athlete's ear," I said.

"Make your goddamn call," he said, but not unpleasantly.

I took out a tan pocketsize address book and made the goddamn call.

It was to Super Joel who owned an art gallery of considerable size and reputation and was quite possibly the coolest place in the city to throw a last-minute party. And we were going to *fucking* party. Like it was 1999.

Or better yet, 1977.

THE NIGHT I GOT DAVID BOWIE LAID *sorta*

— IGGY TO THE RESCUE —

My North Beach flat was a mere hop, skip and a bump away from the Mabuhay, so Jimmy, alias Iggy Pop, would at times drop by afterhours unannounced. The doorbell would ring, I'd glance outside and there below he'd be, looking up at my second-floor window with that big rubbery grin, a cutie on each arm, and I'd buzz them in.

At first glance, one might think my decorator was the surrealist filmmaker, Jean Cocteau. I had this long, butcher block table painted white that had mannequin legs with racy red garters and a television, also white, with mannequin arms. In the middle of this expansive room stood a work of art I titled Stairway to Heaven: a sandblasted door mounted on a white staircase. And propped against a wall was the crowning achievement, a custom-made sofa that, in actuality, was simply the letters S O F A carved out of thick Styrofoam and airbrushed a red-orange gradation.

Jimmy and I would do lines, smoke doobs, and shoot the shit into the wee hours.

(Having said that, not every visitor was into recreational drugs. David "Psycho Killer" Byrne came over one night with Brian Eno, the savvy record producer and rock star in his own right, and using a one-sided razorblade Brian chopped a fresh ginger root like it was a hunk of coke. After steeping in hot water, we sipped ginger tea, enjoying its pleasant "natural high," while singing along to Jackie Wilson, Bobby Vee, and Gene Pitney LPs. It was altogether amazing, but I suppose you had to be there.)

Jimmy was quite the raconteur. You name it, we discussed it. Music, books, chicks, and flicks. Of the latter, his favorite at the time was a sprawling slapstick disaster film called *The Big Bus* and was about the maiden cross-country voyage of a nuclear-powered, titanic-sized Scenicruiser that went so fast it could break the wind barrier.

"You gotta love a bus that breaks wind," Jimmy laughed. If he made a record of nothing but his laughter, it would quite likely chart on Billboard's Hot 100.

He was staying at the Caravan Lodge in the Tenderloin with his girlfriend Esther Friedman. Even though, at least according to one of the Stooges' songs, he wanted to be her dog, she never kept him on a short leash, which is why, on more than one occasion, he'd bed down on my hardwood floor, curled up on the foam letters S and O, an Afghan Hound or two nuzzled up against him. On one such occasion, early in the morning before heading back to the motel, he asked if I was coming to his show that night at the Old Waldorf and I told him I'd love to, but couldn't on account of the Nuns and I had recently been 86'd from said club.

Jimmy liked the Nuns. When they jammed together—or, as I liked to say, Jimmy'd—they truly rocked. It was no secret that his original band the Stooges had greatly influenced the Nuns, as did also the Velvet Underground. In fact, it was said that if Iggy and Nico had a love child, it would be the Nuns. Jimmy was greatly displeased, to say the least, that we got 86'd and wanted to know why.

So, I told him.

The Old Waldorf had booked the Nuns for three nights as the supporting band for Blondie. We were stoked and, to make sure the show drew a sizeable crowd, we rented an outdoor billboard on Broadway right across the street from the Mabuhay to announce the engagement. But then, uh oh. On the first night, an overzealous

Nuns fan had somehow ticked off Clem Burke, Blondie's drummer, which in turn ticked off Deborah Harry, which in turn ticked off the club's owner Jeffrey Pollack. Maybe Blondie wasn't comfortable with the crowd we drew. But what band doesn't now and then draw an unruly fan or two? Some just seem to draw more than others. David Cassidy, the king of teenyboppers, for example, drew far less than, let's say, Siouxsie and the Banshees. But, for the most part, the Nuns drew a diverse crowd that didn't consist entirely of snots and vulgarians. Maybe one of our fans had puked on Clem's drum set. Maybe there was some pushing and shoving. Maybe somebody punched somebody and got punched back. Maybe this, maybe that. There were a lot of maybes. So many, in fact, that the following day I got a phone call from Jeffrey Pollack. No ifs, no ands, no buts, no maybes, the Nuns were being kicked off the bill.

I was understandably stunned because how could any band be held directly responsible for the actions of one or two overzealous fans? But what was even more baffling was this so-called fallout between the Nuns and Blondie. They had always gotten along splendidly. As a matter of fact, a month prior to the Waldorf gig, Blondie and the Nuns plus The Ramones had all stayed at the Tropicana in West Hollywood and, as one might imagine, a good time was had by all.

I still have a clear picture in my head of Deborah Harry, Joey Ramone and Jennifer Miro, the Nuns' keyboardist, lying poolside at 3 p.m. taking their morning coffee and you never saw whiter white folks. It was as if the song "A Whiter Shade of Pale"—though recorded years earlier—had been written especially for them. They were punk rockers, after all, and like vampires their skin hardly ever saw the light of day. It was also pointless their being in such proximity to a swimming pool when the only part of their bodies that dared to get wet was their tongues.

"A vodka tonic, please!" Debbie said, ordering her breakfast.

It was an existential experience listening to Debbie and Joey hold a poolside conversation.

"Whatta douchebag!" Debbie said, referring to somebody she'd met the night before. Evidently, a douchebag.

"Yeah," said Joey with a long, cavernous yawn. "A douchebag."

"A *real* douchebag!" said Debbie.

"*Huge* douchebag!" said Joey.

And so forth. I never bothered to ask if said douchebag had a name. I suppose it didn't matter since just about everybody in Hollywood was a douchebag.

But getting back to the Nuns being 86'd from the Old Waldorf. In way of retaliation, I called Dirk Dirksen and told him we wanted to do a free show the next night—a spite performance, as it were—and to bill it as The Revenge of the Nuns.

"Fuck yeah!" said Dirk. Evidently, there was little love lost between him and Pollack.

That night, we stealthily climbed the rickety metal ladder to the outdoor billboard—the Nuns' roadies Rabbit Jones and Joey Swails, and I, their hands-on manager—and armed with cans of spray paint (while keeping a vigilant eye out for the cops) wrote TO HELL WITH in front of the printed words THE OLD WALDORF. Below that, we spray-painted an arrow aimed across the street and spray-painted: FREE CONCERT SEPT. 21 MABUHAY.

We took a snapshot of the billboard and it wound up in the San Francisco Chronicle alongside a juicy write-up by the esteemed music critic Joel Selvin.

Then came the night of the Nuns' free concert (also the debut of Penelope Houston and the Avengers) and, without doubt, there were a thousand fans lined up along Broadway and all the way down Kearny Street. That same night, meanwhile, less than a mile away at the Old Waldorf, Blondie played to a half-empty room.

"Hey, man, that's completely fucked up," said Jimmy, in no uncertain terms. "Just show up tonight at eight and be waiting outside."

That night I was at the Old Waldorf at eight and, as directed, waited outside.

Inside, the 8 p.m. show was packed beyond its 600-seat capacity.

Outside, the 10 p.m. ticket holders had started lining up, hoping to be as close to the stage as possible when Iggy did his crowd surfing thing.

Little did these Iggy Pop fanatics imagine that a special extra bonus was waiting in the wings, because the star of the show, in full view of everyone, strutted outside wearing nothing but black bikini briefs, combat boots, a German Heer helmet, kohl rimmed eyes and the usual body makeup to shadow and accentuate his Yoga-induced muscle tone. He gave me instructions to stick close behind and marched me inside.

To my unease, we had to walk past the owner of the club, Jeffrey

Pollack. He was standing at the entrance, took one look at me and did a slow burn. I did a coy little finger-wiggle under my chin the way Oliver Hardy timidly fiddled with his necktie. "Uh, uhm," I uh-uhmed. "Hiya, Jeffrey."

That's when Iggy, on his way backstage, stopped, turned, and gave Pollack the classic one finger salute. "Hey, Jeffrey," he said, "throw *me* off the bill, why don'tcha!" He waited a beat, and chuckled. "Didn't think so."

Jeffrey gave him a thin smile. No way, of course, would he dare throw The Godfather of Punk off the bill and be required to refund twelve hundred tickets.

Iggy Pop photo by Robert Altman

So, thanks to Jimmy, I was officially un-86'd. He put his neck out for me. His bare torso, too. Any other rock star would have likely sent a roadie or a girlfriend to walk me in. But no, not Iggy Pop. He was a rock and roll rarity: an authentic good guy.

So, it was not surprising, then, that when I introduced myself as "Jimmy's friend" to Bowie, we straightaway became chums. That, and the fact that I could locate some killer blow put the friendship on speed dial.

EDWIN HEAVEN

— THE PARTY THAT FELL TO EARTH —

Shortly after making the call to Super Joel, I gave the address of our impromptu "Bowie Bash" to David's bodyguard with instructions for David to meet me there at 1 a.m.

The objective, obviously, was to keep the party on the down-low, but naturally somebody couldn't keep their lips zipped, for there were gathered outside Joel's gallery Art for Art's Sake about a hundred or so party crashers. I needed someone I could depend on to man the fortress and that someone was Rabbit Jones, the Nuns' able roadie.

Rabbit was not an intimidating presence but one formidable dude. He was short, about five-three, and not particularly brawny. But, even so, was fearless, the way a pint-size Yorkie will go head-to-head with a heavyweight Rottweiler. He wore his customary short-brimmed military-style cap and a black leather jacket unzipped to proudly reveal a Nuns T-shirt. He clenched a Billy club, which he was not disinclined to use. He bore more than a passing resemblance to rock star Rick Derringer. In fact, when the Nuns headlined the Starwood in West Hollywood, Rabbit and Rick on a whim swapped identities. Rick put on a Nuns T-shirt and, masquerading as Rabbit, performed a few roadie tasks, while Rabbit, impersonating Derringer's swagger, wandered through the crowd warbling "Rock and Roll, Hoochie Koo." More than likely, he relished trading places much more than Rick, because at the end of the night he left with a foxy Rick Derringer groupie. Now that's not to say being a Nuns roadie didn't appeal to a certain groupie element. Just not as many, or as foxy.

And now, there stood Rabbit guarding the entrance to the party, the model of authority as he softly whapped a Billy club into a palm with a slow, steady *thwack, thwack!*

"So, tell me, Heav," Rabbit said, with a thwack-thwack, "who gets in and who don't?"

I hadn't given that much thought, so winged it. "If you know them," I said, "or they know me, let them in."

"Sure, but how the fuck do I know they know you?"

Giving it barely a moment's thought, I said, "Ask them the name of my dog."

"Don't you have two?"

"Which doubles their chances, right?"

"Okay, but what if, you know, she's like real cute and doesn't know the answer?"

I laughed. "*She?* Then ask *her* something easier."

"Like?"

"Oh, you know, like who's buried in Grant's Tomb."

Rabbit held the Billy club like a long cigar and wiggled his eyebrows up and down. "And tell 'em *Groucho* sent her."

* * *

But where were we? Ah—yes—back to smoky places.

The room, by now, looked like the final scene in *Casablanca*, except instead of Claude Rains and Humphrey Bogart shrouded by fog, it was David Bowie and I enveloped by cigarette smoke.

"David," I said, poorly imitating Bogey, "I think this is the beginning of a beautiful friendship, cough cough."

David graciously indulged me with a chuckle, then reached into the breast pocket of his fine leather jacket and pulled out a photo, its edges a tad frayed. A picture he obviously reached for frequently.

"Zowie," he said, showing me the snapshot of a towheaded child probably no older than five.

A chic name for a kid, I thought. "Whatta beautiful boy," I said.

"My finest achievement," he said.

"Considering you have many, that's saying a helluva lot."

He snortled. Then snorted. He looked at the photo one last time before putting it away somewhere next to his heart. "Miss him madly," he said. He took a drag on a Gitanes, expelled a snaking stream of smoke through his Garboesque nose, exhaling the remainder. "You have any kids, Edwin?"

"A boy and a girl," I said. "Ben and Sally." Then thought I should add: "But they're Afghan Hounds."

"A majestic breed," he said. "Dali has one."

"So does Picasso, I think," I said. "And how about you? Got any dogs, David?"

"Not unless you count *Diamond Dogs.*"

*   *   *

Elsewhere, the party was going great guns. *Drive-In Saturday* was blasting from Joel's extravagant speakers. Everybody looked more than a bit starstruck, and rightly so: Mr. Ch-Ch-Ch-Ch-Changes was in the house. But, that's not to say there weren't a few other eminent bands in attendance, including Blondie. While manning the door, Rabbit, or so I was told, had given Deborah Harry a pretty hard time. Acted as if he didn't know who she was. Kept her waiting while others were let in. She knew he was yanking her chain and knew it was some silly retribution for the Old Waldorf incident. She may not have known the names of my dogs, but she knew when she was being punked. When he asked for the name of one of my dogs she replied, "Douchebag?"

Rabbit made the sound of a game show buzzer. "Ehhhnnt! But, you get one more guess."

She took a wild stab. "Fido Fuckface?"

Rabbit sniggered. "Wrong!" But, nonetheless, waved her in with a sweeping gesture. Later, he confided how difficult it was to stay angry with Debbie for very long.

But I digress. Back in the smoke-filled room, David was having a lively discussion about avant-garde filmmaking with the Nuns' guitarist Alejandro Escovedo and his girlfriend Bobbi Levie. Also, in on the conversation were two other members of the Nuns, Jeff Olener and Jennifer Miro. David, the year before, received critical praise for his motion picture debut in *The Man Who Fell to Earth*,

Rabbit Jones, world's sweetest badass

and Alejandro and Jeff, also the year before, tried their hand at filmmaking. It was to be about The World's Worst Rock Band. Al and Jeff, figuring they looked cool enough to be in a band, decided to portray the band in the film—even though, at the time, neither could play a lick. It mattered not, though, since the band, after all, was to be the world's worst.

Jeff Olener, a subway-grown New Yorker sounded like a combination of Lou Reed and Al Jolson and had all the attributes of a rock star. Once, in the backstage men's room at the Whisky, I walked in on him getting an enthusiastic BJ from a top executive at ABC Records. I did a swift one-eighty, but as I headed out the door,

I cracked wise: "Don't just give him head, Susan, give him a record deal!"

Alejandro Escovedo was cool. Steve McQueen cool. That's if the "King of Cool" had been a Mexican, or, at least, had darker skin, hair and eyes, and a penchant for skinny black jeans and pointy-toed boots. Being from a large family of talented musicians—Pete Escovedo, Coke Escovedo and Sheila E., to name but a few—he miraculously, nearly overnight, turned himself into a raw power guitarist along the lines of the Stooges' James Williamson.

While Al and Jeff were casting the rest of the band at a rehearsal studio, they fortuitously came across Jennifer Miro, an alluring keyboardist and songstress. At the time, she was in a Doobie Brothers cover band, along with Mike Varney, an accomplished musician and terrific bass player. After Jenny and Mike, came Rafael, a more than competent drummer, and Richie Detrick, a Sal Mineo lookalike with a booming voice to share vocals with Olener and Miro. And thus, the Nuns were born. But, unlike the fictitious band in Al's little film—the so-called "worst band in the world"—the Nuns were to become the direct opposite. In fact, the night I first saw them—they were opening for the Ramones at the Mabuhay—I thought them so astonishing, I signed them on the spot.

I wouldn't have been there that first night if not for the tenacity of Jennifer Miro.

Jenny and I had met the previous year at Bimbo's 365 Club after a Tubes show, a band I promoted and, on occasion, got up on stage and performed with—in particular, on their phantasmagoric grand finale "White Punks on Dope." (Years later, there was a Tubes reunion at the Rio Theater in Santa Cruz and midway through "White Punks," I turned to lead guitarist Roger Steen, whose mic I was sharing, and between frantic gasps asked if the song had gotten longer. "No," said Roger, "we just got older.") After the Bimbo's show, Jenny and her girlfriend came back to my apartment and even though it was her girlfriend I got it on with that night—a pretty little redhead with inverted nipples that, when stimulated, would become erect making it a lovely game of hide and seek—it was Jenny who stayed in touch, calling me like every other month or so. "Edwin," she'd say, "come see my band." She did this over and over until, finally (and fortunately), I did.

Jennifer Miro stood well over six feet in heels and that first night I saw her perform, oh what a sight. She walked onto the stage like a fashion model on a catwalk. A platinum blonde with blood red lips dressed in gothy black lace like a Morticia Addams. She sat at the keyboard, her spine erect, holding her body as tall as possible while bathed in a white spotlight. The rowdy crowd hushed the moment she began to sing in a come-hither contralto. Think husky Marlene Dietrich meets sultry Peggy Lee.

> *I'm laaaazy, so lazy, I'm too lazy to fall in love*
>
> *It's such a bother, I'd much rather stay home and watch TV.*
>
> *It's such a bother, such a bore*
>
> *The same old lines you've heard a million times beforrre . . .*

At the song's conclusion, the stage lights flashed an apocalyptic red and white as out sprang five darkly clad toughs. Someone counted off—*1-2-3-4!*—and they flew into their bombastic set. Like a game of Duck Duck Goose, Olener, Detrick and Miro swapped vocals. What made the Nuns so unique, so explosive, was not just their eclectic repertoire or their hooligan ways, but also the amalgamation of rowdy street toughs and a towering baroness. Not for a moment was I bored. I was hooked and reeled in right up through their anthemic closing number.

> *My suicide child, my suicide child*
>
> *Cross the mile on the dirty filthy bathroom tile*
>
> *Walked on by, I was so high*
>
> *My suicide child, why did you die?*

To say I was blown away would be an understatement. I didn't just walk backstage, I zombie-staggered and in a cramped room with wall-to-wall graffiti, mostly obscenities, I straightaway announced

I would be their manager. The mood was jubilant as we clinked bottles of Bud as if it were flutes of Dom Perignon. It would be several months before I discovered punk rock bands, by and large, are unmanageable.

* * *

Al, Bobbi and Jeff left to suss out the rest of the party, but Jennifer stuck around to chat up David. When he mentioned he and Iggy were rooming together in Berlin, her eyes went so wide her long lashes nearly stabbed her eyebrows.

"I love Marlene Dietrich!" she exclaimed.

Now, I, too, was a fan of Fräulein Dietrich but if Berlin came up in a conversation my first thought wouldn't have been her. The Third Reich, maybe. Or the Berlin Wall, perhaps. Or possibly its great film directors: Fritz Lang, G.W. Pabst, and Ernst Lubitsch. But David seemed enchanted by Miro's pronouncement. So much, in fact, that he let slip that he would soon be making a film with Marlene Dietrich.

Iced water usually flowed through Miro's veins, but, at that moment, it was blistering bouillon.

"I'm playing a handsome gigolo," he said offhand. Then added, humbly, "Which is definitely casting against type." Then he let drop that this gigolo gets to screw Kim Novak on the floor.

"Lucky gigolo," I said. Then, not nearly as humbly, I divulged that, although I never screwed Kim on the floor, once on a flight to Hollywood we had misbehaved.

Miro was gaga. "You . . . Kim Novak . . . Mile High Club?'"

Before I could utter an *au contraire*, David quipped, "Did you get *Vertigo?*"

A clever double entendre, since it was now hardly a secret that David was aviophobic. They say people who live with fear are only living half a life, but whoever said that obviously didn't know David Bowie. For clearly his cup runneth over. And it's a pretty big cup, or so legend has it. Earlier that evening he had told me how he much preferred crossing the Atlantic by luxury liner and traveling from city to city in a stretch. To accommodate this more leisurely, less stressful mode of touring, management would book his concert dates a good number of days apart. He liked to stretch out in the back of a limo, strum a guitar, write songs, read books, watch TV— and sometimes bring along a travel companion. If he tired of her company, she got a plane ticket home and many a fond memory. I imagine he also carted along an ample supply of contraband. Pot, booze, ludes and the ever-popular "Zhivago"—a term, incidentally, I coined. One night after a Tubes show at Bimbo's 365 Club, I met

Julie Christie, the exquisite star of *Doctor Zhivago*, and invited her back to the band's rehearsal studio—along with her friend Gerrit Graham (who played Beef in De Palma's *Phantom of the Paradise*), Boz Scaggs and his wife Carmella (who, along with unspeakable beauty, also possessed the wit of a Dorothy Parker and the figure of a Sophia Loren—"A real stacked tomato," she'd say)—and, of course, various members of the Tubes, including "The One, The Only" Prairie Prince, drummer extraordinaire. Someone, I forget who, laid out a few fluffy white lines that resembled snow and I handed the mirror to Julie and said, "A line of Zhivago?" She laughed, then partook and, in all probability, brought the neologism back to Tinseltown where, a few years later, a very young Quentin Tarantino would use it in the screenplay for *True Romance* as a dealer's code word for cocaine. ("Lee," says the character Clarence, played by Christian Slater, on a payphone, "the reason I'm talking with you is I want to open *Doctor Zhivago* in LA and I want you to distribute." Lee, the movie producer played by Saul Rubinek, replied warily, "I don't know, Clarence. *Doctor Zhivago* is a pretty big movie.")

But, once again, I've digressed.

"You and Kim Novak? On a plane?" Jennifer Miro was blown away by the unforeseen nature of her artist's manager. "Oh, Edwin, please! Tell-all! You simply must!"

David, with a bad-boyish grin, mimicked Jennifer. "Yes, Edwin, you simply must!"

And so I did.

Back when I was producing rock concerts at the Monterey fairgrounds, my partner Marguerite Gaffney and I, on a United flight to Burbank, had just buckled our seatbelts and were waiting for the last passenger to board, when who should that be but none other than Hollywood sex goddess Kim Novak. Even in faded blue denim she exemplified Va-va-voom (with a capital V). She was looking around for a seat and noticed one that was vacant between me and Marguerite, who patty-pat-patted the cushion and said, "Kim, dear, come join us." Of all my friends, Marguerite was probably the most enlightened. She read a lot of Krishnamurti, for starters, sometimes she'd drop acid at bedtime then wake up hours later peaking, and was tenderhearted by nature and would use terms of endearment such as "honey" and "dear" and "darling" and "angel" when addressing even a stranger. Kim gave Marguerite a quick once over. She was wearing a semi-transparent white blouse and in her long auburn hair was a white lily. She looked like a well-to-do flower child. Then Kim gave me a fleeting glance just to make sure I wasn't The Boston Strangler. I was dressed all in leather, a nifty fringe doeskin jacket and black suede bellbottoms. I had an Afro sorta like Hendrix (but without the headband) and a fashionable moustache. She smiled like I was William Holden and scooted into the unoccupied seat.

As the plane began its takeoff roll, I was sitting with a leg crossed over the other and she placed a hand on my thigh and gently uncrossed it.

"If the plane was to suddenly brake," she explained, "wouldn't want to lose the family jewels, would we?"

"No, we wouldn't," I said, her hand lingering a second or two longer than expected.

"Taking off always makes me uneasy," she said.

"Depends on what you're taking off," I said, then immediately wished I hadn't made such a dumb joke. I was greatly relieved when I heard that husky laugh. Maybe it wasn't such a dumb joke, after all.

When the plane reached cruising altitude and we had loosened our seatbelts, Marguerite took out a small pewter pillbox, unlatched it and, using the teeniest silver spoon, took a whiff of a pale lavender powder, then casually offered it to Kim. "It's mescaline," she said, "would you like some?"

To my amazement, Kim took the pillbox and teeny spoon. "I've always wanted to try it," she said, then discreetly—or as discreetly as a major motion picture star could possibly be on a commercial plane at practically full capacity—took a whiff.

Then, yawp! The pillbox and spoon was offered to me.

I was momentarily indecisive, being slightly claustrophobic and not exactly wild about flying to begin with, and worried that intensifying my sensory perception with a psychedelic might snowball my anxiety. But, only a schnook would wuss-out while seated next to a 35mm goddess who had costarred with many a Hollywood hunk. So, I sucked it up and took a whiff.

And cowabunga! The three of us were now flying higher than the friendly skies of United, yet not quite so high that I got vertigo. Although, for a split second, I saw Alfred Hitchcock seated across the aisle making one of his famous cameo appearances, but the hallucination soon turned out to be just a rather plump middle-aged woman with a double chin and thinning hair.

Then, rather unexpectedly, her hand was in mine, and this time I wasn't hallucinating. It wasn't the soft, smooth mollycoddled hand of a Columbia Pictures A-lister. It was a rugged, calloused hand of (as I would later find out) an equestrian, but would've felt pretty nice even if it had been a catcher's mitt. (Obviously, the mescaline was doing its thing.) I wanted to tell her I had a crush on her since I was twelve, but fortunately didn't. She would've most certainly taken her hand out of mine.

"So, tell me," Kim said, "are the two of you headed to Hollywood on business or pleasure?"

"Meeting agents, booking bands, talking to potential investors,"

Marguerite said. "We're producing rock concerts, me and Googy."

Kim grinned and gave my hand a squeeze. "*Googy?*"

I must've turned calamine pink when she laughed. Then we all laughed, but we probably would've laughed if someone had merely said something like Chevy hubcaps, or aardvark, or ooh eeh ooh ah aah ting tang walla walla bing bang. Yes, we were that high.

"And you, Kim?" asked Marguerite. "Business or pleasure?"

"Oh, most definitely pleasure," she said. "Gonna go play with Frank and Sammy."

Of course, she could mean only one Frank and Sammy, but feeling lightheaded and goofy, more so than usual, I said, "Frank *Shufflebottom*, the plumber? Sammy *Schmangelwitz*, the kazoo virtuoso? Hey, I know them, too!"

For whatever reasons, she liked my ridiculously dumb jokes and laughed like I was Mel Brooks. It was a very psychedelic laugh. Seemed to reverberate like she had a wah-wah pedal in her belly. But instead of a wah-wah, it was a hah-hah. Egods, we were high. And so completely blissed-out, that not till the wheels touched down in Burbank did we stop laughing or let go of each other's hand.

Inside the airport terminal we said our goodbyes, exchanged phone numbers—Marguerite and Kim made a date to go horseback riding—and we headed off in opposite directions, Marguerite and I toward the Hertz counter, Kim toward a waiting limo.

I hadn't yet come down from the mescaline and I was sure she hadn't either, so I glanced back just to check on her.

"You okay, Kim?"

She turned and gave me that tough-as-nails stripper's smile, the one from *The Man with The Golden Arm.* "Yes, I'm okay. Are *you* okay—*Googy?*"

"Oh yes!" I said. "Good god, yes!"

She blew a kiss and walked away, hips in blue jeans swaying side to side, off to party with Frank and Sammy.

And I'm not talking about Shufflebottom and Schmangelwitz

David, charmed, asked if he could deliver a message to Kim.

"Yeah," I said. "Tell her Googy has yet to touch ground."

Jennifer spotted someone she had dated, Crime's talented drummer Brittley Black, who resembled a combination of Tony Curtis and Soupy Sales. She hastily excused herself and hurried to catch up with him.

Soon as she left, yet another member of the Nuns walked in, arm in arm with Dee Dee Ramone. When Richie Detrick lived in New York, he and the Ramones' bass player were roommates and lovers.

"Wassup, Edwin? Wassup, David?" They were both wasted. Dee Dee, in particular. Quaaludes, perhaps. "I hear it's snowin' katzenjammers in here," Dee Dee said.

Whereupon, Super Joel poked his head into the room. "Just checking to see if there's anything you needed, David. Besides an air purifier or an oxygen breathing apparatus."

But wait, allow me digress once more.

I first met Joel Tornabene a couple years prior when he showed up at the Boarding House nightclub for the Tubes' Talent Hunt, the same anything-goes event where a still-undiscovered Robin Williams—wearing furry cowboy chaps and a brassiere over a hairy chest—got the ol' vaudeville hook. Super Joel also got the ol' heave-ho. His "act" (though we didn't know at the time it was an act) was heckling. If there had been a heckler contest, he would've won, but, as it was, he got tossed, which only endeared him to the Tubes.

He was also, I might add, a notorious political activist. There's a famous Pulitzer-winning photo of a protestor placing the stem of a daisy into the barrel of a national guardsman's rifle. That gallant young man, purportedly, was Super Joel.

Accompanying Joel into the room was a bearded biker fondly known—at least to most—as Dirty Al. (I use "most" as a qualifier on account of he was murdered the following 4th of July. Neighbors ignored the gunshots, sadly mistaking them for firecrackers.)

Art: Prairie Prince   Concept: Edwin Heaven

"Dirt" passed around a joint every bit as plump as he was. It was quite potent and, my guess is, it was either Maui Wowie or Thai Stick, although it packed such a wallop it might as well have been called "George Foreman." Zapped and pummeled as we were, David and I looked around, simultaneously, for a chair to plunk our sorry asses upon. Joel, the perfect host, pulled up a couple cozy chairs as someone (at this point, I was too stoned to make out who) pulled out a pocketknife. I darted a glance at David's bodyguard expecting him to haul ass across the room and shield his boss with a barrel-sized chest, but the pocketknife merely dipped its bitty blade into a gram size polyethylene bag and packed Dee Dee's nose. The sight of it reminded me of the time I saw Mick Jagger using a very long dagger to scoop up some coke and then, adroitly, placed the razor-sharp pointy tip no less than a nostril hair beneath Ron Wood's proboscis, a juicy morsel I right away shared with David.

"We called it The Jagger Dagger," I told him.

"Too funny. I must share that one with Angie."

I didn't ask why but, having read a British tabloid or two, had a hunch. Plus he had mentioned earlier that he and his wife Angie, from the very start, had enjoyed an open relationship.

Meanwhile, "Mr. Pocketknife," whoever the fuck he was, offered a tootski to Richie, who passed, so Dee Dee merrily did Richie's toot, too. Then, the two tootle-oo'd and when Dee Dee was halfway to the door, I called out: "Stop thief! Stop! Po-lice!"

Dee Dee turned, chortled, and said, "Open the fucking door!"

I noticed this tete-a-tete between us had piqued David's interest.

"Let me in on the joke," David said after Dee Dee's exit.

"Okay, but I'm gonna warn you, it's gonna mean having to endure another fucked up anecdote."

Using the ember of a finished Gitanes he lit another and said, "The more fucked up, the better."

And so I began: "The last time I partied with Dee Dee Ramone, I was lucky I didn't land in the slammer."

It was the beer run from hell.

"Hey ho, let's go," Dee Dee said. "Before the stores close."

It was nearly 1:30 a.m. and the party was in a dodgy neighborhood. It was unthinkable to go in search of a liquor store on foot, but, fortunately, a friend, Menno Meyjes, had a Volkswagen Beetle and was not opposed to driving one of the Ramones to a store. So, hey ho—off we go!

I was immediately impressed with the legroom in that little VW Bug. Menno, perhaps the Netherlands' tallest screenwriter, didn't look the least cramped behind the wheel. Couldn't say the same, though, for Dee Dee in the back seat. So, when we came across some mom and pop liquor store South of Market, the neon "Open" sign still lit, Dee Dee wanted to be dropped off, posthaste. We found a parking spot halfway up the block and thought it best to lock the doors. Although, if a gang of hooligans wanted to, they could easily pick up the VW Bug and carry us away. While waiting for Dee Dee to return with a couple six-packs, we nattered about what scripts we were currently working on. I was adapting an uproarious, sexually explicit adaptation of *Young Lust*, an underground comix, for Alan Douglas, the Jimi Hendrix producer. He had already received letters of interest from John Belushi and Gilda Radner. Menno was working out of Francis Ford Coppola's office nightly, from midnight till morn, on *The Children's Crusades* which years later would evolve into Spielberg's *Indiana Jones and the Last Crusade*. He was in the midst of describing the opening shot—four and twenty blackbirds fly out of a gigantic pie—when, suddenly, there's a bang-bang-banging on my window causing us to nearly jump out of our skin, like a couple slapstick comics in an old-time movie.

"Open the fucking door!" Dee Dee screamed.

He was holding a large, filled grocery bag while yanking the door handle. I was just about to unlatch the lock when I heard, coming from a distance: "Stop! Thief! Stop! Police!" I glanced in the side rearview mirror and there, down the street, an elderly Asian, possibly Korean, was shouting at the top of his lungs. "Stop! Thief! Police!"

"What the fuck?" Menno and I said to one another almost in unison, as Dee Dee continued to bang away on the window.

"Did he just rob that store?" asked Menno.

"We let him in, we'll be accessories to the crime!"

"You'll be an accessory," he said, "I'll be the fucking getaway driver!"

"Jesus Fucking Christ, guys," Dee Dee yelped, "let me the fuck in!"

The old man was relentless. "Stop! Thief! Police!" If he suddenly had a coronary, along with theft we'd be charged with homicide. So, against my better judgment, I opened the door and in shot Dee Dee, headfirst, into the backseat. Tumbling everywhere were pretzels, chips, beer, booze and Twizzlers. He preferred the strawberry kind.

"Stop! Thief! Police!"

"That old guy could give Freddie Mercury a run for the money," I said.

"Hurry!" Dee Dee yelled, as distant sirens grew louder. "Step on it!"

Menno's foot stepped on the accelerator like it was a cockroach but the little Beetle with its rear-mounted air-cooled engine was no muscle car.

"Go go go GO!" Dee Dee Ramone shouted like he was counting off "Blitzkrieg Bop"—*One-two-three-four!*

As the VW finally picked up some speed, the old man's screams were drowned out by Dee Dee laughing his foolish punk ass off.

"And so," I said to David, "Menno reluctantly became the C.W. Moss to Dee Dee Ramone's Bonnie and Clyde."

"You're right, that was really fucked up," he said. "What I don't understand is why he would rob a store in the first place?"

As I rolled around in my head the question of Dee Dee's motives, a cute brunette in a slinky black dress standing in the doorway seemed to catch David's eye. Actually, both of them.

"I rather fancy that one," he said sotto voce.

It wasn't the first time that evening I noticed how this charismatic personality could be painfully shy. So, undertaking the role of wingman, I called to her, "Hey, hello there!"

"Groucho sent me," she replied.

I chuckled and gave the bodyguard the okay sign.

She came over and I introduced the two of them, thusly: "Berlin, David. David, Berlin."

"Berlin," David said as if it were the name of a fein spätburgunder. And right before my eyes, any shyness I had earlier detected suddenly vanished, as if timidity was just another one of David's many personas.

— BERLIN, AGAIN —

I met Berlin at a Marilyn Monroe lookalike contest. She was a contestant, I was a judge. She was second runner-up, which sounds impressive, for it's no small feat beating out a score of would-be glamour queens, until one discovers the first runner-up had a full beard. Albeit, it was platinum, but a beard, nonetheless. For runner-up Alan Flamingo's talent demonstration, he performed a dance routine in *Seven Year Itch* drag surrounded by young men dressed in Yankees uniforms, their Louisville Sluggers painted a glittery puce. Mr. Flamingo's effort, alone, was worthy of second prize.

But all contestants paled in comparison to 19-year-old Janet Sean. From her platinum blonde waves to her pouty red lips, her copious cleavage to her shapely booty, if not the spitting image of

Marilyn Monroe, she was damn close, closer than anyone else. She brought down the house with her whispery rendition of "My Heart Belongs to Daddy" serenaded to a life-size cutout of Clark Gable. The following year, she would move to Paris to become Salvador Dali's model.

Janet Sean (far right) posing with the Tubes
Photographer: Mikel Covey · Art Director: Edwin Heaven

Berlin, on the other hand, even with a blonde wig and clinging black gown, only somewhat resembled MM. The truth was, she looked more like Betty Boop. But Berlin had all the classic Monroe poses down pat—the sinuous stance, the bare arms flung upward—and her smile was both saucy and innocent.

And now, sans blonde wig, Berlin had won a far grander prize:

the full-undivided attention of a rock god.

"Berlin," David said her name once again as if relishing a luscious wine, "were you by chance listening in on Edwin's story?"

"Guilty," she said, eyes downcast.

"Splendid!" he said. She lifted her gaze and looked at him with openmouthed wonder. "Then, please," continued David, "perhaps you can illuminate us as to why Dee Dee Ramone would rob a mum and pop store?"

"I should hazard a guess?"

"Precisely," he said, sounding a bit like Professor Henry Higgins.

"He was thirsty, he was broke," she said after giving it no more than a moment's thought.

"Thirsty, maybe," I said. "But he had cash. I know for a fact because we all chipped in."

She shrugged. "Then maybe it was, you know, the punk thing to do."

David and I were not altogether convinced, so she proposed one last theory.

"Maybe," she said, addressing me, "he wanted you to write about it. You and your friend both being writers and all."

Pantomiming his fingers typing on a phantom typewriter, and sounding a bit like me, David said, "'What a badass motherpunker

Dee Dee Ramone is.'" Then laughed. "Oh, Berlin, you're bloody brilliant!"

So, there you have it. Not only was she kewpie-doll-cute, she was smart as a whip. And David, the "Little Toy Soldier," fancied whips.

Noticing there were sparks between them—and having exceeded my threshold of nasal cavity abuse—I decided to call it a night.

"Ta ta, cheerio, David," I said. "Auf wiedersehen, Berlin." But as I started walking away, he put a hand on my shoulder.

"Don't know if you're headed home or just going to the loo," he said, "but I want to thank you, mate."

"For what?"

"For this lovely party."

"But, David, like I said . . . *you're* the party."

As I headed toward the door, I could hear Berlin explaining— much to David's amusement—our little in-joke about Groucho sending her.

"Then Groucho is a bloody angel," he said.

* * *

— BERLIN, AGAIN AND AGAIN —

Woke up feeling like shit. Took three days to recover. A malaise I henceforth call the Three-Day Bowie Flu. I vowed that morning to never smoke another cigarette or do another line—at least, not as many lines. When I was fully recuperated, I rang up Berlin, picked her up in a cab, and whisked her off to a flick. Fittingly, Truffaut's *The Man Who Loved Women.* Then drinks afterwards at Enrico's, the famous sidewalk café on Broadway. After her second Pink Squirrel, she let drop a bombshell. As she lay bare the titillating details, my jaw dropped like the Big Bad Wolf in "Red Hot Riding Hood"—the Tex Avery classic cartoon—and, for all I know, my lower jaw is still laying there on Broadway.

In the back of the limo, en route to the Hyatt Regency, they made out feverishly.

"He may have been a Limey," said Berlin, "but his tongue was totally French."

"Leave it to Berlin to turn the Thin White Duke into a thin white frog."

"By the time we stumbled into his suite, I was wet as San Francisco Bay. At high tide."

"Were there fog horns?"

"Just whistling."

She went on to explain that as she lay there, sprawled across the king bed, stripped to her panties, the tide rising (figuratively speaking), David was in the bathroom whistling.

"Whistling what?"

"Not sure," she said.

"Remember how it went?"

She couldn't whistle, so she hummed a few bars—*ta-ta-ta tah dum, ta-ta-ta tah dumm*—which I vaguely recognized as Wagner's "Ride of the Valkyries." Replicating all those trumpets, oboes and bassoons is no small feat for a whistler. But Bowie wasn't just any whistler. Although, I thought it odd as his choice of mood music, waiflike Berlin was no Brünnhilda.

"Then, came David's grand entrance!"

The bathroom door flew open and out he came, wearing nothing but his boots. His hair wet and slicked to one side, strands cascading over his left brow. He held the tip of a black pocket comb over his upper lip to resemble a small rectangular moustache. And with an extravagant "Achtung!" he leapt onto the bed and goose-stepped around her, his right arm rigid in an outstretched salute. Then, with a boot planted on each side of her, and with a stereotypical German accent, David Bowie declared, "I've alvays vanted to screw Berlin!"

And needless to say, he did.

Multiple times.

EDWIN HEAVEN

1964

THE EXOTIC OLDER WOMAN

"Googy, there's something you gotta know," she said, as I unzipped her, "and I hope it don't send you running for the hills."

What hills? We're in Atlantic City. The town is sea level. Literally.

Behind her, the wallpaper had a seahorse motif that made her look submerged. The room, rented per week, was a stone's throw from the Boardwalk, that's if you had an arm like Roberto Clemente. The salty breeze mingled with the savory scent of Taylor's Pork Roll chargrilling less than a block away. And the rhythmic lapping of waves did a duet with some new girl group on the radio singing about some burnin', yearnin' feelin' deep inside and how it hurt so bad. Whenever I got that burning feeling deep inside, I simply took an Alka-Seltzer.

"But if it does make you run for the hills," she continued as I unfastened her Maidenform bra, "I won't blame you, not one bit."

"Rosalie, there's nothing you could tell me, nothing that could possibly turn me off." I said this dangling the bra like a black lace slingshot and feasted my eyes on its previous occupants. "Unless, of course, you're about to tell me you have a dick."

Her dress lay around her waist and I reached under it. It felt moist as morning dew and I let out an exaggerated sigh of relief.

She laughed, slowly removed my hand, resting it on a warm, smooth thigh, and said, dead serious, "I'm married, Googy."

I was not entirely bowled over by the news, nor was I surprised. For one, I had already met her little daughter that afternoon. And while Rosalie hadn't been wearing a gold wedding band, she had on a diamond big as the Ritz—the Nabisco cracker kind.

"And I think it's only fair," she said, "you oughta know what you're getting into."

I can't wait, is what I almost said, but instead said nothing as she went on about the hubby and how, back when they first met, he was driving a truck and how by the time the kid was born he owned a fleet of them. Owned her, as well.

Then, she said he's in with the mob and paused to weigh my

reaction.

Truth be told, the fact that I hadn't lost my erection was a miracle in and of itself. And it didn't go unnoticed.

"Hmm," she hmm'd. "Evidently, mobsters don't scare you."

"Not in the least," I lied.

* * *

Back in the '50s, my dad owned a cocktail lounge in Hollywood, Florida called The Vogue Room. It had become a favorite haunt for many a made man. Due, in part, to its proximity to the jai-alai frontons and the Hialeah dog track, but partly, also, because the barmaids had spectacular bosoms. I was just seven or eight and was particularly fond of Ginny. She was kind, liked kids—or, at least, liked me—smelled real good and, as I mentioned, had great bazooms, the kind that belonged in a 3D movie. A snapshot she gave me was stowed in the secret compartment of my Hopalong Cassidy imitation-leather wallet, like it was a prophylactic.

After school, I hawked a five-cent local rag called the *Hollywood Sun-Tattler*. "Extra, extra! Read all about it! Liz Taylor gets married again!" Whether Liz did or didn't, didn't matter—it sold newspapers. But, what sold the most papers was stepping into The Vogue Room to say hello to my dad, Ginny and the genial gents who had lots of loot to spend. Bookies, racketeers and mobsters in pastel blue blazers, dark shirts and light ties, tan and white wingtips, daffodil-yellow slacks with a crease running down the front, pressed-linen pocket hankies, fedoras worn cocked to the side and tilted slightly forward (they dressed this snazzy even in the light of day), and every so often they'd buy my entire batch of *Sun-Tattlers*. After all, I was Artie's kid. And Artie played golf with "The Crime Minister" himself.

Everyone seemed enthralled by this crime boss except my mom.

"Art," she said, "I don't like you playing golf with that man."

"What man is that?" I asked as I polished my father's three-wood—a club he was as proficient with as he was with a blackjack.

"Costello," my mom said, making a face as if she was saying impetigo or head lice.

"Costello?" My favorite comedy skit of his was Who's on First. "Is Abbott gonna play, too?"

Dad chuckled and mussed my hair. "Not *that* Costello, Goog."

"*Frank* Costello," Mom said, again with the face. "A meshuggeneh mobster."

"But a damn good golfer," Dad said. "And a real nice guy."

"Nice my tuchis," Mom said. "One day you're going to hear something you shouldn't, Artie. Get yourself killed."

"Marcy, it'll never happen," he said in that charming, lilting way of his, especially after he had a few. "I make him laugh!"

"Ha! I wonder how many jokesters he's got buried in a sand trap somewhere."

And now that I think about it, Mom was quite the jokester, too

* * *

Her husband being in tight with the mob wasn't the only bomb Rosalie dropped. Her previous boyfriend—the one the husband called "*melanzana*"—had been whacked.

"Chopped up," she said, "and dumped into the ocean."

Suddenly, she had my full attention—which was not easy, being that my dick was also at attention.

"Because of the color of his skin?"

"He probably would've gotten clipped even if he'd been white," she said. "Or purple. A jealous husband sees only the color red."

Blood red, I'm thinking.

"So, Googy, like I said, you wanna make a run for it, sure, I'd be sad, but I wouldn't blame you one bit."

Inside my head I could hear a Greek chorus chanting: *Run, Googy, run!* With the Crystals, maybe, singing backup: *Da doo run-*

run-run, da doo run-RUN!

Fastening her bra and escorting her out the door would've probably been the sane thing to do. So, why didn't I? Maybe because I was twenty, she was twenty-six—the Exotic Older Woman. Not to mention, she was fucking unbelievably gorgeous. But the best explanation for not doing the rational thing was something my dad told me when I turned thirteen: *Son, when the pecker is hard, the brain is soft.*

* * *

It had been lust at first sight.

I was bopping along the beach, catching a few extra rays before heading off to work, and that's when I saw a sylphlike, copper-tanned goddess in a pink bikini. As was the fashion: light blue eye shadow—heavy on the eyeliner—pale shade of lipstick and lashes out to there, lashes as long as Twiggy's. A jet-black bouffant completed this picture of an Italian Cleopatra. And, as stated earlier, she was fucking unbelievably gorgeous. The drop-dead kind. Or, maybe, I should say, the found dead kind.

"Gina! Gina!" she called to a little cherub probably no older than four.

This was my shot, and I took it.

"*Gina, Gina,*" I sang, doing a half-decent impression of Johnny Mathis, "*I kissed you once and then, I felt so wonderful, so very wonderful, let's do it over again.*"

Gina giggled and spun around and around in the sand. Her mama flashed a Pepsodent smile revealing slightly crowded teeth, which, ever since that summer's British Invasion, I found oddly attractive. I envisioned that extraordinary mouth agape as she moaned in ecstasy, her body shuddering orgasmically, and on a frequent basis, if I had anything to say about it.

She brushed sand off the beach towel, which I read as an invitation. "Hello," she said, extending a sandy hand. "I'm Rosalie."

"Googy," I said, taking her hand and, on impulse, kissed it like I was the Count of Monte Cristo Sandwich.

"Is Googy the name on your birth certificate?"

"Yeah," I said, wiping grains of sand off my bottom lip. "Right after the words: Do Not Believe."

And so it went. She'd say something and I'd make some stupid joke. Not that I was particularly stupid, it's just that her smile was a huge turn on, and I was determined to keep her smiling. Whatever I was doing seemed to be working. And when she handed me her tube of Bain de Soleil and rolled over on her belly, I didn't put up a fight. Smeared that orange goop everywhere not concealed by her bikini, which was about 95% of her. I ran my hand over that superbly slim body while, around us, kids screeched, tossed quoits, twirled hula hoops and, overhead, a single-engine plane hummed as it towed a banner: CAPTAIN STARNS—SEAFOOD & SEA LIONS!

When I was done, she glistened and purred. So did my hand.

A vendor, lugging a white box suspended by a leather strap around his neck, shouted, "Get'cher Fudgie Wudgies! Ice cold Fudgsicles!" He was shirtless—wore his white t-shirt on his head like an Arab—and was a talented kibitzer. For instance, he hollered to a pregnant sunbather, "I got the *'sicle*, you bring the *pickle!*" When he was within twenty feet, he quickly noticed Rosalie (how could he not?), and with showman skills lifted the lid to the cooler, reached into the depths of the foggy dry ice and extracted an ice cream sandwich that he lobbed in her direction. Acting on instinct, like it was a foul ball at Shibe Park, I snatched it out of the air and gave it to little Gina. Rosalie started rummaging through her purse, but the vendor waved her off. "It's on the house, mademoiselle!" he shouted. Like she was Brigitte Bardot. "Anything for a beauty queen!" Then off he schlepped, the beach his vast Sahara. "Ice cream sandwiches! I supply the *'wich*, you supply the *sand!*"

It wasn't long before Gina's hands dripped vanilla and with that chocolate cookie mess on her chin she looked like a pint-sized beatnik. "Gina, go wash up," said her mom, and the kid scampered off in the direction of the ocean to splash her sticky little hands in the shallow waves. "Keep away from the older boys," Rosalie shouted when she noticed bodysurfers crashing into unwary bathers. Then added, "And watch out for the jellyfish!"

"Unless it's covered with peanut butter!" Me and my stupid jokes.

"And don't go no further than you already are, young lady," she yelled. "A wave could carry you off!"

"I'd like to carry you off," I said, intimately, thinking this might be a good time to make a move.

Our lips practically touching, she said, "Don't mess the hair."

"The kiss is supposed to mess up the hair," I said to her luscious mouth, "the hair isn't supposed to mess up the kiss."

"Tell that to my hairdresser," she said just before we locked lips. It was the Swinging Sixties, after all, and stuff like this happened in a heartbeat.

And so, there, hidden behind a large beach umbrella, we made out. Long and hard. She long, me hard. Her supple tongue nearly touched my uvula. My already-too-snug bathing trunks suddenly felt two sizes too small. Her eyes fell upon the bulge, its outline clearly defined. The only thing left to the imagination was the mohel's signature.

"You're Jewish?"

I laughed. "Only from the waist down."

She was a doting mom, but not the most attentive—for which I'll take a portion of the blame—but she quickly remembered there was a small child left unattended.

"Oh geez!" She looked over to where Gina had been playing footsies with the seaweed, but the child wasn't there. "Gina!" she screamed. "Oh geez! Gina!"

But, thankfully, there she was, little Gina peering around the beach umbrella.

"Mommy kissed Cookie! Cookie kissed Mommy!"

I had to be at work in a half hour, no time to dilly-dally, but, even so, I sang a couple bars from the Mathis song "Gina," which made the little munchkin giggle and, once again, spin around and around. I then asked Rosalie if we could meet up later when I got off work at ten, but she had promised Gina a sleepover at her "Nonna's"—an hour's drive—and she had never broken a promise.

Maybe I looked crestfallen, or she maybe was as hot for me as I was for her, because she said she'd try to make the drive back to the shore. I did the Mashed Potato right there in the sand, my schlong did The Frug.

Told her I worked at Shumsky's, the Romanian restaurant on

Pacific. She said she'd driven past it and asked if the "cuisine" was any good.

"If you like kosher-style," I said. "But the pineapple cheesecake is to die for."

Then, from out of left field, she asked if I would die for a woman.

Keeping it light, I said, "Only if she was covered with pineapple."

Back in my room, there was no pineapple topping, but I did keep a stick of Dentyne under my pillow, so that the first thing upon waking I could chew it and have morning sex without the "morning breath." But, had I known of the dangers that lie ahead, I would've also kept under my pillow a gun.

* * *

The diners, a few locals but mostly tourists and conventioneers, had come and gone, and at ten I took off a gravy-speckled apron, tightly bundled it into a ball and jump-shot it into the laundry bin.

The Two Joes, as they were called, were gaping out the window at a candy-apple red '64 Cadillac DeVille convertible parked out front, its top down. The portly Joe was the barkeep and, with his black oily hair parted down the middle, bore a striking resemblance to Jackie Gleason's comical character Joe the Bartender. He even sounded like Gleason. *How ya doin', Mr. Dennehy?* The other Joe, not the least portly, was a waiter the others aptly called The Other Joe. But it wasn't just the swanky car that held The Two Joes' attention. No sirree. Behind the wheel sat a sexpot of godly proportions. Her black strapless gown fit like a second layer of skin and laid bare tanned shoulders more sumptuous than anything on Shumsky's menu, even the cheese blintzes & sour cream. Even the cheesecake!

The Two Joes took her for a Bond Girl.

"Wonder who she's waiting for?" said Joe the barkeep.

"Sean Connery."

"Or Dr. No."

"If was me she was waiting for," said The Other Joe. "I doubt I'd ever take *no* for an answer."

"That's called rape," I said, slipping a slice of pineapple cheesecake into a doggie bag.

"And that's called larceny," said The Other Joe.

"Then we're all thieves," said Portly Joe, patting his beer gut. He then shifted his attention back to the hot Italian broad in the Caddy. "She sure as hell ain't waiting for some lowly busboy, that's pretty obvious."

I grinned. "Good night, gents," I said, taking my leave and my cheesecake.

Once outside, I bounded into the Caddy DeVille the way I

imagined Errol Flynn would have, and presented the cheesecake to my "Maid Marian" as if it were the finest long-stemmed roses freshly cut from Sherwood Forest. We kissed ravenously, as if apart for years, like I had just returned from The Battle of Okinawa—her tongue sweetened by the pineapple topping. I managed, somehow, not to mess her hair. Out of the corner of my eye, I could see The Two Joes, their faces pressed against the window glass, staring stupidly. So, I waved. Rosalie gave the horn a couple soft taps—as if to say "ta-ta!"—and with the Beatles twist and shouting on the radio, away we drove into the star-studded night.

I suggested we grab a drink at The Opus One, a local nightspot that was in with the in-crowd and tucked away in an alley off the beaten track, but she nixed it. Apparently, the hour-long drive back from her mother's had, in no way, diminished her penchant for driving and, I suppose, if I owned a spanking new Cadillac ragtop, I, too, would want to take my new squeeze for a spin. Twenty marvelous minutes of laughing, fondling, and singing along with the radio and we're at Tony Mart's, a waterfront bar in Somers Point, dancing, drinking and rubbing bodies in the dark, smoky nooks.

The emcee, WMID radio deejay "Hairy Barry" Richards, who dined regularly at Shumsky's (and the following month would be taking me to see the Beatles at Convention Hall), was broadcasting live from the club and when he spotted me in the crowd, spoke into the microphone in a mellifluous baritone: "Great googa-moogy, it's mah man, swoogy Googy!"

I shot her a glance. Was she impressed? One thing for sure, Hairy Barry was.

All through the night, not once had Rosalie allowed me to pay for anything. Not even a Singapore Sling. In all probability, she sensed that the tips of a busboy didn't amount to a hill of beans, let alone a couple Singapore Slings.

Not till we were alone in my room later that night, when she spilt the beans about the demise of her former boyfriend, did I fully comprehend her motive for driving all the way out to Somers Point for drinks. It was to stay clear of Atlantic City nightspots and the risk of running into one of her husband's "goombahs." Or, worse still, running into her husband.

So, there we were, in my sparsely furnished room, that new Motown girl group on the radio singing about their "baby, baby" and "where did our love go." I had more than a sneaking suspicion where Rosalie's last love went: to the bottom of the ocean, in bits and pieces, courtesy of her louse of a spouse.

And, oddly, upon hearing this most discouraging information, there I was still, her bra in hand, ready, willing and able—emphasis on the able—because, as I previously mentioned, when the penis is hard, the brain is soft. And mine was a toasted marshmallow. I sat there on the edge of the bed transfixed by her glorious half-nakedness, her breasts impervious to childbearing. Not a droop nor a stretchmark, her dusky pink nipples perked with expectation.

We kissed, and then we kissed some more. She probably sensed, having had more experience in these matters, that I was a tad gun-shy, so she unbuckled my belt, unzipped my fly and freed willy! She paused to take it all in, then she took it all in, and not just figuratively.

She engulfed the entire cock and caboodle. Licked it from knob to nuts. To an unworldly twenty-year-old—who till that summer of '64, lived with his grandparents while commuting to campus—it was as good as it gets.

As great a pleasure as it was, her giving me head, my desire to please her was as great. So I maneuvered, careful not to dislodge my "Fellatio Alger" from her splendid mouth, and lowered her panties so my tongue could reciprocate. But when I began to lick her, she wriggled away.

"Oh baby, I'm sorry, but not tonight," she said. "I'm having my monthly nosebleed."

Earlier at Shumsky's, I recalled one of the waiters discussing his girlfriend's period and saying how he liked a little ketchup with his steak. And, although it sounded cool at the time, the way he said it didn't sound particularly romantic. But now it did. So, I did what any man in my position would do. Whined and begged.

And just like that, we're right back in the heat of things.

While she was giving extraordinary head, I slipped off her panties, spread those silky thighs and—oh fuck! There was one more little snag. A white string dangling. Though adept at unhooking bras and unzipping zippers, never had I removed a tampon. Upon closer inspection (although I guess you couldn't get any closer than I already was), I concluded it wasn't unlike skydiving—or, in this case, *muff*-diving—so I did what any diver would do: I pulled the ripcord and, Geronimo! It glided out with the greatest of ease. A quick glance at the tampon revealed the "nosebleed" had mostly diminished. And so, my will to please dampened not in the least, I dove right in. One might say, that as she licked my dick, I dicked her with my tongue. Like I was licking jelly inside a donut.

When she shifted her position and got a glimpse of my mouth, she giggled.

"Looks like you got on lipstick," she said.

I wiped my mouth using the back of my hand and on it was a smudge of blood. Reddish-brown. Like a red velvet cake. Cakes and donuts, I was ravenous by now.

"Yum," I said.

"Umm," she said, guiding me inside.

I was in deep, you could say, in more ways than one. And we were off to the races—except right out of the gate I was about to cross the finish line. I pulled back the metaphorical reins by shifting my thoughts from her sweet damp to something not the least sexy. Like Willie Mays racing around the bases, his cap flying off. Or visualizing a truck-driving Al Capone kicking down my door. And it worked! Ejaculation effectively forestalled. Now, once again back in the saddle, we galloped in a dead heat. I gave her my best moves, she gave me hers. Like anthropomorphic Slinkys, our bodies twisted and bent into a myriad of positions, natural and unnatural. We were The Fucking Aristocrats! Not to get too explicit (as if I haven't already), but this I must disclose: hers was an unbroken succession of orgasms. If it were one of those old-timey theatrical trailers, the word COMING! would be flashing on and off the big screen. (Or perhaps, if not thought too tacky, it would be spelled CUMMING!) Each of her orgasms seemed to swell in magnitude, the decibels increasing histrionically until she was screaming at the top of her lungs. And she had a nice set of lungs. I was more than somewhat concerned the other tenants might think someone in my room was being beaten to death and they'd call the cops. Or worse, call the hubby. Which is why, whenever she would resoundingly express immense pleasure, I had to muffle the shrieks by placing a pillow over her face and, it got so, I worried I might smother her.

If only she had come and gone. A wham-bammer. Ships passing in the night. Arrivederci, bellissima Rosalie!—and, while we're at it, shalom, auf wiedersehen and sayonara! (After all, we had gone "around the world.") But such would not be the case, of course, because I, for one, could not get enough. Nor could she. Put it this way: if she were an all-you-can-eat buffet, I would, in no time, become one of those sideshow fat men.

We had done the deed—a fait accompli—and now there was no turning back. And since you can't put the Pepsodent back in the tube, might as well keep on squeezing. We didn't think we were morally or ethically in the wrong (or so we rationalized) since her husband's murderous ways eclipsed her adultery. But no doubt about it, we were aware that what we were doing was most certainly, unquestionably hazardous to our health. Particularly mine. We were like two kids playing with fire. A high wire act without a safety net. Two love-happy elephants galumphing across a minefield.

Oh yes, it was wrong what we were doing, but it felt oh so right.

*   *   *

It was Dentyne time. I reached under my pillow for the stick of gum, gave it a few quick chews, did a breath check making certain it was cinnamony fresh, and kissed Rosalie lightly on the lips.

"Good morning, Sleeping Booty."

Her eyes fluttered opened and, savoring my tongue, murmured, "Mmm, gimme some a dat."

Like a robin feeding a chick, I transferred the partially premasticated gum. She gave it a couple quick chews—the gum, not my tongue—then wrapping her arms and legs around me, I glided inside. After a night's rest I was prepared to go all morning. But such would not be the case. The sex was rushed on account of she needed to pick up the kid. The good news, however, was she'd be driving back that night. Contingent, of course, upon the probability that her husband would still be away on business.

On the beach that afternoon, as I soaked up the rays, I replayed the events of the night before. Replayed it several times, in fact, and, subsequently, when I arrived at work I still had a boner.

Until Johnny Shumsky, wearing a serious face, pulled me aside.

"Googy," he said, "your days as a Shumsky's busboy are over. Done. Finito. Kaput."

Was I being busted for pilfering a tiny slice of cheesecake?

"Geez, Johnny . . . it was crumbled and smooshed and would've wound up in the bus box anyway. C'mon, Johnny, I'll gladly pay for it."

"Pay for what? What the fuck you talking about?"

"Uhm, what are *you* talking about?"

"I'm talking about we can't have anybody who's dating a gorgeous piece, like the one last night, clearing tables and schlepping bus boxes."

"But I busted ass as a busboy and—"

"*And*—" He cut me off like so much foreskin at a bris. "Now you're gonna bust ass as a *waiter!*" With a big grin, he shook my hand like I'd just been bar mitzvahed. "Congratulations, boychik!" Then he called to the bartender, "Joe, give Googy a waiter's jacket. Assign him a station. Take him into the kitchen, let chef know Googy's now a waiter. You know, give the kid the lay of the land." Then once again to me, he said, "Speaking of the lay of the land, what's the cheesecake's name?"

"Pineapple."

"Her name is Pineapple?"

"No, uhm, Rosalie."

"Well," he chuckled, "tell Rosalie if I wasn't a married man—" He stopped dead midsentence when he noticed Mrs. Shumsky—The

Dour Empress of Kishka—standing within earshot. "A very *happily* married man," he added wisely.

I suppose I could've told him Rosalie already had one married man in her life to contend with and, as far as I was concerned, one was one too many.

It didn't take long before the dining room filled with the frenzy of chatter and laughter, the slurping of matzo ball soup and the uninterrupted clinks of forks on large white porcelain plates.

One customer, a real wisecracker, was eating sweet-and-sour beef tongue with great enthusiasm, when suddenly he yipped, "I bit my tongue . . . *twice!*"

Everyone at his table had a hearty laugh. An alert busboy raced over with ice cubes wrapped in a napkin to stop the flow of blood, only to discover the customer had merely been kibbitzing. Which gave rise to more laughter.

Meanwhile, I, the rookie waiter, rushed hither and tither, from kitchen to table, table to bar, like a chicken liver without a head of cabbage, carrying three heavy plates on one arm—boiled beef flanken topped with red horseradish, sauté whole chicken livers and onions, broiled jumbo lobster tails with drawn butter, and, of course, the best damn cheesecake in all the land—and did it without spilling a drop of the jumbo Manhattans which I nimbly balanced on a cork-lined tray.

Toward the end of my shift, as I was counting my tips (the louder, more hectic the room and the busier the bar, the bigger the tips), The Dour Empress of Kishka handed me a Guest Check stub, upon which the following phone message was scribbled: *Meet Rose and Lee at Jerry's Ribs.*

Rose and Lee? . . . Ohh, Rosalie!

By the time I clocked out, I was what old-timers would call blotto. Here's why: first, Joe the bartender made me a double Bombay Martini, which in an effort to get out of there in a hurry I might've downed a bit too hastily. Then, as a celebratory gesture for "surviving" my first night as a waiter, Tyrone the prep cook and Juan the dishwasher coaxed me through a fire exit into a side alley and, crouched behind some garbage cans, we shared a plump hand-rolled cigarette. Mary Jane, Juan called it. And, as it turned out, she was Jamaican. Up until then, I had always thought the only people who smoked reefer were beatniks, jazz musicians, Lenny Bruce and the Puerto Rican gang in *West Side Story*. At first, I must admit, I was fearful of being turned into a hophead. But, immediately upon that very first puff (which, dear reader, as you well know, would not be my last), and for no particular reason, I started laughing. Everything was fall-down-funny to me. For instance, Tyrone farted—one of those long foghorns, not exactly sophisticated humor (not even if it were an Oscar Wilde fart)—and Juan applauded, shouting as if at an opera, "Bravo! Encore!" and Tyrone, obligingly, gave us a repeat performance. Even tossed in an extremely loud "curtain call" that had me doubled up in laughter.

The upshot: I was so blottoed, that not for the life of me could I recall how I wound up on Kentucky Avenue. Had I walked those six long blocks or had I been airdropped? But, somehow, there I was, in the heart of Atlantic City's black entertainment district, strolling (or was I floating) through the rib-gnawing crowd in search of the lovely and delicious Rosalie.

She picked the rib joint as a rendezvous, I'm reasoning, because there was less a risk of running into you-know-who. Or anyone who *knew* you-know-who. But it didn't speak to logic. Why would a suspecting husband like you-know-who rule out Atlantic City's black-populated Northside if his wife's last flame (the o ne he allegedly whacked) was black?

Heads turned as Rosalie hip shimmied toward me and slipped into my arms. She was wearing another one of those strapless dresses, its hem ending well above the knee. This one, a fluorescent yellow, not a color one would especially wear if incognito. But, here she was, the center of attention. To say this woman was anything less than spectacular would be like saying the sun was no brighter than a 60-watt bulb, or Babe Ruth only hit singles.

She stepped up to the take-out window and ordered ribs for two. Or, as she called them, "bones." Across the street, an electrified sign shaped like an eighth note read "Club Harlem," but it was the name on the marquee—Sam Cooke!—that charged the evening with electricity. I'm thinking soon we'll be pickin' pork from our teeth and twistin', twistin', twistin' the night away.

While she nuzzled my neck, I couldn't help but wonder if this was where she had also hooked up on the q.t. with the previous loverboy. I also wondered how her husband got wind of the affair. Were her orgasms so vociferous it carried clear across town? Maybe all the way to South Philly?

The slabs of ribs arrived, stacked on white bread to sop up the barbecue sauce. Having smoked that heady Jamaican, my appestat was through the roof. I started to salivate like one of Pavlov's dogs (Rin Tin Tinsky?) but before I could dig in, she grabbed my arm and muttered, "Come quick!"

"Right here? On Kentucky Avenue?"

I was slow on the uptake and she was quick to notice. "Baby, whatever you're stoned on, right about now I could use a toke, myself."

She tossed a twenty on the counter and, still clutching my arm, whisked me across the street.

"Rosalie," I said, "is there something the matter? You seem a little upset."

"I'll tell you . . . when we're alone inside."

She headed directly to the big fella standing at the door, ignoring the long queue in front of Club Harlem.

"'Lo, Ro'," said the big fella. "Long time no see."

"You're looking fit, Bo," she said. "Shed a few pounds?"

"Was a piece-a-cake," he said. "Literally. I now stay the fuck away from cake." Then dropping the smile, he said, "Sorry to hear 'bout Sonny."

So, *that's* the name of the flame who got snuffed. Sonny.

Bo looked at my ID, rolled his eyes as if it was obviously fake, but stepped aside and unhooked the red velvet rope. As I walked past, he leaned in and said in a low voice, "Next time, I confiscate."

"Thanks, Bo," I said, grateful he hadn't.

Inside, it was immense and jam-packed. Looked like the club had something like seven bars with customers standing four deep. The orchestra was riffing Louis Jordan's "Is You Is Or Is You Ain't My Baby" as we weaved through the crowd. When we squeezed past the stage, the drummer did a snappy paradiddle on the hi-hat cymbal and clearly winked at Rosalie. She, in turn, blew him a kiss. She then pulled me into the powder room, pushed me into a stall and, for a muddled moment, I thought this is what she had in mind when she whispered in my ear, "Come quick!"

But no such luck.

"Look, there's probably nothing to be concerned about," she said, pulling out a tube of lipstick from her purse. "But, just in case, go along with me on this." She began applying it to my lips. "Trust me on this, Googy."

"Tell me you're not serious."

"Last night, when you were, uh, pleasuring me, then looked up at me with those blood red lips, I was struck by how, uh, pretty you looked. Then just now, actually when we were crossing the street, the idea hit me. So go along with it, Googy, no matter how batshit crazy it seems."

When she was done applying the lipstick, she took out eyeliner and, as she's applying it, just to show you how batshit *blotto* I was, I'm thinking: *If wearing a little lipstick and eyeliner turns her on, then so be it.* (And this was a decade before the arrival of glam rock.)

Then like a cold splash of hydrochloric acid, she said, "Maybe he spotted us, maybe he didn't."

"He?" I said, sobering quickly. "He who?"

"A colleague of my husband."

Which was another way of saying we're in a life or death situation. Good thing I was standing close to a toilet, less chance of crapping my pants.

"Maybe he wasn't tailing us," she said in a lackluster attempt to console me. "Maybe, you know, he's just into soul food. And, let's face it, it don't get much better than Jerry's Ribs."

"I wouldn't know," I said, picturing those succulent ribs I had to abandon. And the thought occurred to me that I might not live long enough to find out how succulent.

"Aw, Googy, it's not that bad, we're just playing it safe," she said, putting away the eyeliner. "And by safe, I mean act as though your queer."

I realized, the moment I stepped out of the stall, that inhibiting my sexual proclivity would be a difficult task. I was standing in a powder room paradise. A fine, fine, superfine woman was shaping an Afro with a long hair pick. Another—quite leggy, her skirt lifted—was adjusting a garter belt. And a top-heavy black beauty, braless, wrestled with a zipper, allowing for a brief glimpse of an enormous tit. I say *brief* on account of when I took a step toward her to help with the zipper (like any gentleman would, heterosexual or not), Rosalie spun me around, steered me toward the exit. Glancing in a mirror, I pursed my red lips and batted my lashes.

"Don't overplay it," she said. "We'll meet at the bar, the one in the back. Make mine a Manhattan. Get yourself something chichi with lots of cherries and maybe a little pink umbrella."

She gave me a pat on the ass and off I went. The route to the bar was clogged with clubbers in various states of inebriation. It took some jostling, a little zigzagging here and there, but finally I bellied up to the bar. Before I could order, though, as if by magic, two drinks appeared before me: a chilled Manhattan and a multicolored highball served in a frosty zombie glass with a pineapple-cherry garnish sporting a miniature pink parasol. Whether in the sack or in a nightclub, Rosalie never ceased to amaze. I had no idea how she pulled that off, unless if in the ladies' room there was a cocktail waitress taking orders with a walkie-talkie.

Somebody pinched my ass. The price, I suppose, for getting all dolled up in a smoky, darkened nightspot. I turned, ready to conk the guy, but it wasn't a guy.

"Hey, slowpoke, what took you so long?" Rosalie said, as if she'd been waiting there since the repeal of prohibition.

"Apparently, there's a shortcut I didn't know about."

"It's called a straight line," she said.

All of a sudden, she looked down, as if she spotted a fly drowning in her drink.

"Don't look now," she said out of the side of her mouth, "but here he comes."

But, of course, I looked. And 'here he comes,' indeed: a thug in a sharkskin suit and highboy collar, his tie the only thing about him that was skinny. He looked like the CEO of the Human Pretzel Company. From the pompadour to the dagger-sharp shoes, the message was unmistakable—Warning: Thugs Can Be Harmful to Your Health!

As he approached, he cleared a path for himself, shoving clubbers out of the way. One didn't take kindly to being pushed and looked like he was about to do something—something stupid—until, that is, he caught a glimpse of this thug's face, which looked like it had been stung on the nose, chin and forehead repeatedly by angry giant wasps.

"Rosalie!" he said in a surprisingly high-pitched voice. Almost a castrato.

They did one of those cheek-to-cheek air kisses. Then, he said in that piping voice, and not the least concerned about being overheard, "This is some spooky joint. Gives me the fuckin' willies." He looked around. "Where's your friend? The sexy little blonde used to go wid you on Bandstand. Cunny?"

"Connie."

"Yeah, the one usually rides down to the shore wid you. She here?"

"She's got a date tonight. And, gee, I didn't know she was your type."

"My type?" He laughed. "Tits and ass, that's my type."

"Next time I'll be sure to fix you two up," she said, laughing hard. Harder than I ever made her laugh, and I should've been jealous except I knew she was faking it.

"Thanks, doll," he said, turning his attention to me. "And who the fuck is this?"

"A friend," she said.

"Boy friend?"

"Of course not, silly. Me and Googy, it's strictly plutonic."

"Well, Pluto better not be poking Minnie while Mickey's away."

"Not to worry," said Rosalie. "If it was up to Googy, Pluto would be poking Mickey."

"Me and Rosalie, we're more like *girl* friends," I said, with just a trace of swish. (After all, didn't want to overplay it.)

"Googy's my protectress," she said.

Apparently, he, too, was a bit slow on the uptake. "So that's not grenadine on his lips?"

"It's Revlon's Love That Red." I said with a flicker of flirtation. "And who are you? Burt Lancaster's stunt double?"

"I'm Sal's pal," he said.

"You're pals with Sal Mineo?"

"Sal's my husband," Rosalie explained, as if I needed one.

He extended his big paw for me to shake—hell, I was prepared to do the air kiss thing, if need be—and said, "Friends call me Worm."

I tittered, "Hate to think what your enemies call you."

He tightened his grip on my hand, gave me a long hard look. It was too late to take back the remark. I gulped my cocktail. The tiny parasol nearly poked out an eye, to which he let go of my hand and let out a shrilly laugh. He wasn't pissed in the least and was only fucking with me.

"Looks like you're the one could use a protectress," he said, and we all laughed. Then to Rosalie, he said, "When I spotted you across the street, I thought it would be rude not to come in here and pay my respects."

"I'm glad you did, Wormsy," she said, although to me it was clear she wasn't. "I know Sal appreciates stuff like that."

"That said," he said, "got some bones across the street getting cold and nobody likes a cold bone." They did the air kiss thing again. "Ciao bella."

He gave me a parting glance and I fluttered my lashes.

"You oughta see a doctor about that twitch," he said, and left the same way he came in, using muscle to clear a path. What I imagine he does for Sal, and then some.

I heaved a sigh, picked up a cocktail napkin and started to wipe off the lipstick, but she stopped me. "No, keep it on," she said.

"But you heard him, he's not coming back, this place gives him the willies."

"I'm not worried about Worm. Right now all he's thinking about is my friend Connie and all the crazy ways he's gonna please her."

"So why shouldn't I wipe it off?"

"It turns me on."

"Well, that's a good enough reason for me," I said, and lifted my glass. "Here's to many a turn-on." And many a hard-on. We clinked glasses, and downed our drinks.

When she went to the powder room to powder whatever needed powdering, big Bo the bouncer came over and, as before, leaned in close.

"You must fuck like a champ," he said.

That night, though, I didn't.

What happened was, she said we ought to play it safe, and she wasn't talking about condoms. Said she had to drive back to her mom's to avoid further suspicion. I, too, thought it wise, but told her I would worry about her driving all that distance at such a late hour.

"I'm a trucker's wife, what's fifty miles?" She snapped her fingers. "It's like a trip to the corner store."

*   *   *

Knuckles on the door woke me much too early. Mrs. Rossi, most likely. Rent was paid a week in advance and the landlady paid a visit every week to collect. It's said that a tenant once skipped out on her and she vowed never would another. ("Them's the rules, young man," she said like a matronly John Wayne, back in early June when I took occupancy.)

"Okay, okay, be right there!"

But, instead, I lit a Winston and, holding it between the lips, wriggled into my jeans. Upon removing the cigarette, I noticed lipstick traces on the filter. Revlon's Love That Red. I must've crashed the moment I stumbled in and, evidently, didn't wash up. A peep in the mirror also revealed I still had on eyeliner. Oh well, what the hell, it's just the landlady, no big thing, so I opened the door.

There in the hallway stood someone a lot beefier than Mrs. Rossi. He was closer to her age than mine, with thinning hair slicked back on the sides like he had just run a wet comb through it. Even though it was the middle of summer, he had on a well-worn leather jacket. Though he spoke soft and whispery, there was an immediate air of toughness about him.

"I'm Sal," he said.

My dark summer tan must've turned a ghostly white, like in some cartoon.

"Maybe you know me?" he said. "We know the same people."

I become jokey when panicky. "John, Paul, George and Ringo?"

"Rosalie," he said, pushing me aside, and walked in like he owned the goddamn place. For all I know, he did.

It occurred to me I hadn't emptied my bladder since the night before, and having a purported murderer standing within choking reach of my throat significantly increased the urge to urinate, but didn't think it wise to leave him unaccompanied in my room. I stood there holding it in while mulling over the prospects of not making it through the morning in one piece, and said, all swishy and flirty, "Ro' said you were a 'man's man' and, man oh man, she sure as hell wasn't kidding."

I might as well have been chatting up a crocodile.

"When I got back last night," he said, "I drove out to the mother-in-law's to surprise Gina. You know Gina?"

It was rhetorical, so I simply nodded and smiled.

"She was asleep, the little angel, and I didn't wanna wake her," he said. "So, I stuck around thinking I'd surprise my wife, figured she'd be home soon enough. But, was not the case. You can imagine how any husband would be more than a little concerned, y' know, his wife not being home and all. So, I got ahold of Worm. You know Worm."

Again, with the rhetorical, but this time, as I nodded, the smile wilted.

"And I find out," he said, "she was last seen with you. But Worm was quick to add I needn't worry on account of you being queer."

"As a three-dollar bill," I said, half-curtsying.

"But then Gina, when she wakes up, tells me somebody named 'Cookie' kissed her mommy on the beach. I didn't know queers went around kissing mommies on the beach. I thought only daddies."

Short of sucking his dick, I was determined to keep up the gay ruse. "Is that why her daddy dropped by?"

"You know the fuck why I stopped by." He said it in that whispery way but it terrified me, so he might as well have shouted it.

Somehow, I found the composure to snub out my cigarette

with a steady hand. "Your wife and me, Sal, are like sisters," I said, a limp wrist for effect. I knew (even back then) that portraying a gay man so stereotypically was reprehensible, but when your life is on the line, fuck subtlety. If Sal suspected I was straight and banging his beloved, I'd windup alongside Sonny, her previous loverboy—chopped like liver and dumped into the Atlantic. "It's strictly a girly-girly thing," I said. "Nothing romantic. Maybe, now and then, she'd be like a wingman, point out a cute guy to me and say, 'go get 'em, tigress.' That's the straight dope, cross my heart and hope to die." I immediately realized, of course, that "die" was perhaps not the best choice of words to use at that moment.

His eyes swept over the close quarters as if in search of something to bear out my self-proclaimed gayness. But, alas, there were no hot-pink short-shorts scattered about, no giant wall posters of bare-chested men or, for that matter, a Liberace candelabra.

The room's best feature, aside from its proximity to the beach, was its full-sized mattress, upon which I had schtupped his wife and now silently prayed he wouldn't peel back the top sheet and discover—perish the thought—a smirch of menstrual fluid. If he did, though, I would own up to having a bleeding hemorrhoid.

"Got something in this Playboy Mansion to drink?"

"Just some spigot water."

"Fuck."

"Is that a yes, Sal?" This riveting banter was interrupted by more rapping on the door. "That's the landlady coming around for the rent," I said, and headed toward the door. Remarkably, he made no effort to stop me from opening it. And no wonder. Into the room burst Worm, still wearing what he had on the night before, his pompadour gone limp.

"It's not him, Sal," he said in that piccolo voice.

I was relieved—or at least as relieved as someone with a bladder about to burst.

"But, Sal," Worm said, "what I gotta tell you, you're not gonna fuckin' love." He then delivered the news about as delicately as a stampeding rhino. "She spent the night wid another *mulignan!*"

It was as if Worm's screechy announcement had bounced off the walls, sailed out the window and clambered up the stairs before reaching Sal's ears, that's how long it took for Sal to react. And when he did, he spoke even softer, more whispery.

"Who?" he said, like a two-hundred-pound wounded owl.

"He plays the drums at Club Harlem."

Yawp! I should've known. If she'd cheat on her husband, what was stopping her from cheating on me? But then it occurred to me: maybe what she did, she did for me. Throw off the trail. Save my sorry ass.

Then, on second thought . . . *naaah.*

"So whadaya want me to do, Sal?" Worm said and slammed a fist into a palm. "Break his face?"

Sal gave it hardly a thought. "Beat it like a drum," he said, matter of fact, like he had just ordered a hoagie and not a hit.

He then turned and took a couple steps toward me. Instinctively, I took a couple steps backward.

"What are we doing here? The fucking Two-Step?" He said this with a grin. It softened his features, made him look more like the kind of guy who'd bounce a baby on a knee, not someone who'd knee someone in the nuts before bouncing him down the stairs. Having narrowly dodged the latter, I considered myself most fortunate. "You don't mind, pal, if we pass on the spigot water," he said, pulling out a wad and peeling off a Benjamin. "Here," he said, handing me the crisp C-note. "For time and trouble."

"Anytime, Sally," I said, smoothly sliding the C-note in the waistband of my jeans, like some male stripper. Then, uncontrollably, I started to do that little slinky dance kids do when they gotta pee so badly their teeth are floating like lily pads. I guess it came off like I was Salome doing The Dance of the Seven Veils, because Sal turned to Worm and said, a lot louder than a whisper, "Let's get the fuck outta here. Before the vice squad arrives."

I quickly closed the door behind them and made a mad dash into the bathroom, unzipping my fly with such urgency I nearly nicked my dick, and took what surely was the longest, most satisfying leak of my life. And as I stood there, pissing like Seabiscuit, I pieced it all together: after Rosalie had dropped me off at the rooming house under the pretense she'd be driving all the way back to her mom's, she, instead, circled back to the club where, in all likelihood, she had another drink or three and wound up between the sheets with Drummer Boy—who, I'm fairly certain, paradiddled her cooch till the cock crowed. Maybe it even played "Topsy, Part II."

Though my feelings and ego were hurt, I didn't bear any grudge. After all, it was the sexual-liberated sixties, and everybody was fucking everybody.

A couple nights later, as I'm getting off work, there parked outside Shumsky's was the candy-apple red Caddy and, naturally, pressed against Shumsky's window ogling Rosalie were The Two Joes.

"Christ, Googy, by now you must be cummin' orange juice," said Portly Joe. "Or a spicy marinara."

"Hey!" squawked the other Joe in disbelief. "She just gave me the fuckin' finger!"

Amused, I asked, "Her right or left hand?"

"The right."

"Oh," I said as I headed out the door, "then it's not her 'fucking' finger."

When I got into her car it wasn't a finger she gave me, it was a tongue. She was wearing a blonde beehive wig. As long as she was behind the wheel of her big, long red Caddy, it wasn't much of a disguise.

We rode in silence. That's if blasting the radio is considered riding in silence. And as we dined at some remote candlelit bistro, there wasn't much in the way of conversation, either. Nothing had changed on the surface. Rosalie was still drop-dead gorgeous. It's just that I felt not nearly as daffy. Maybe it was her dalliance with Drummer Boy, but who was I to judge? Or maybe it was because I had met Sal, and even though it sounds inconceivable that I could like such a brute, I couldn't help feeling a trickle of empathy. After all, hadn't we both been cuckold by the same woman?

When the waitress placed the bill on the table, Rosalie, predictably, reached for the check. But not before I did. "Googy, I can't let you pay for it. You're saving for college."

"But it's not me that's paying for it," I said, and placed Sal's crisp hundred-dollar bill on the table. "Your *husband* is."

You could've knocked her over with a canary feather.

After that night, we drifted apart. What had begun with a bang ended with a fizzle. We never even exchanged final goodbyes. Maybe because, like that lush golden oldie by The Flamingos, *lovers never say goodbye . . . goodbye . . . goodbye.*

Is this the author formerly known as Googy?
(Atlantic City, summer of '64)

* * *

EDWIN HEAVEN

1969

SO, UH, ARE YOU EXPERIENCED?

This black dude with a stars and stripes bandana wrapped around a 'fro was slouched, legs akimbo, on the beer-stained carpet in a seedy motel watching a Phillies game and smoking a fat joint while a Twiggy-thin groupie with itty-bitty titties was giving him head.

I was standing in the doorway and from my vantage point she sort of looked like a blonde bobblehead. This rather pleasant view was suddenly obstructed by a string-bean rocker with a frizzy 'fro, not quite as cool as Jimi's but not bad for a white boy.

"Ello, mate," said Noel. "Jimi would like to do this interview thing later, like right before the show. Okay?" He said all this in a cheery Brit accent while eyeballing Lolly, a stunning six-foot, big-bosom blonde I had brought along to take photos. I wasn't born yesterday. If I couldn't get a foot in the door, she could—and if not a foot, an enormous titty.

"Okay," I said to the world-famous bass player, trying to sound obliging, though, in truth, I was more than a bit put out. It would've been so cool to kick back on the motel couch and watch the ballgame with Jimi and bandmates. Ask them stuff on the fly, like has Hendrix ever chipped a cuspid while playing guitar with his teeth? Or ever consider selling Jimi Hendrix Musical Dental Floss?

Noel gave Lolly the once-over, once more. Guess you could call it the twice-over. "So, we'll see you tonight at the Spectrum," he said, mostly to her. I sneaked a peek over his shoulder and Jimi seemed more interested in the ballgame than what was going on down around his balls. And for all we knew, he was moaning because his team was losing.

So— there we were, backstage at the Spectrum where a number of the *Rocky* films would one day be filmed. Seating capacity 15,000. And it's a sell-out crowd—a *stoned* sell-out crowd. Even the backstage area was hazy with hashish. Lolly had one hand clutching my arm, the other clutching a Leica M4 with a wide-angle lens. Obviously, she was impressed by my rock and roll prowess. When I had asked, the day before, if she'd like to come along, shoot some pics, she enthusiastically replied, "Oh wow! Jimi Hendrix!" And I had a gut feeling that after the show tonight my arm wouldn't be the only part she'll be clutching.

But, there was a human refrigerator standing guard in front of Jimi's dressing room.

"Excuse me," I said, as I tried to step around him.

"Whoa!" he said, blocking my pathway.

"Jimi said it's okay."

"Woo—he did, did he?"

"Yeah," I said, nodding. I looked over and Lolly was nodding along. Apparently, so were her boobs since Fridge was giving them a long, hard look. She gave him a winsome smile, but he wasn't looking at the smile, he was more knocked out by her knockers and, for a split second, I detected a slight warming, thought maybe The Fridge was thawing.

"Well, in *that* case," he said, now all friendly-like, "if Jimi said so, well then I'll just tippy toe aside, let you two stroll right on in."

"Right on!" I said, but no sooner had I taken a step forward, his palm—big and thick enough to catch a speeding hockey puck—rose to an inch of my nose.

I'm awful at detecting sarcasm.

"Aw, c'mon, cut us a break," I said. "We're supposed to be in that room right now. Ask Jimi. Or Noel or Mitch. Go on. Ask them."

"I already got my instructions. Let nobody in. Nobody. Not even Richard Fuckin' Nixon."

"Especially Richard Fuckin' Nixon," I said, but he didn't crack a smile. Hell, I doubt he would smile even if Lolly (still clutching my arm) lifted her King Crimson t-shirt. Apparently, not only was he the size of a Frigidaire, he was every bit as frosty. He was all business, and his business was making sure nobody—not even Tricky Dicky or, for that matter, Mahatma Gandhi (and especially *me*)—would enter the almighty green room while the boys in the band were chopping and snorting their blow.

"So? You two gonna step away from the door?" Fridge said it softly but it might as well have been through a bullhorn.

"But Jimi—"

"You're not gonna let this go, are ya?"

Only slightly less deflated than The Hindenburg, we trudged off. And, as we did, she removed her hand from my arm, along with any hope of my getting any nookie after the show. To top it all off, I had been hired to do this interview and, without one, I was up the ol' creek without a paddle, or a paycheck.

Then, suddenly— the place is abuzz.

I turn and see the dressing room door is, now, wide open. And in an instant, we're nearly trampled by a stampede of hysterical hangers-on who, just a moment ago, were acting so fucking cool and aloof. Friends and family of the promoter, groupies and deejays, the hipper-than-thous, all wearing their precious laminated backstage pass suspended on a lanyard like it was a SWAT badge, or the pope's pectoral cross. And they were nudging and shoving, trying to get as close a view as possible of Jimi Hendrix, Noel Redding and Mitch Mitchell a.k.a. The Jimi Hendrix Experience as the famed power trio burst out of the dressing room, their nostrils packed with white energy, holding high their weapons of choice: a Fender Stratocaster, a Fender Bass V1, and Regal Tipped drumsticks, respectively. Their roadies and toadies plowed a narrow pathway through the crush.

And that's when Noel spotted me—well, actually, spotted the tall buxom blonde—and, to Jimi, said, *"There* they are!"

Jimi stopped, came over. "Hey, where were you guys?"

With a nod at Fridge, I said, "Rosy Grier, over there."

"Well fuck that shit," said Jimi. "C'mon," he said, motioning with his white Fender as if it's King Arthur's Excalibur for us to follow. "I'll give ya somthin' to write home about."

The backstage mob parted like the Red Sea and Hendrix was Moses, and, like the Israelites, Lolly and I followed him into the arena, through a clamorous packed-house, and toward the circumcenter where awaited a round revolving stage and an array of multicolored floodlights.

Jimi, personally, sat us stage right, where we sat right on the edge, right below those twin towers of Marshall amps. Not only would it change my life overnight, it would also, quite dramatically, alter my auditory system. For weeks after, I walked around just a little less deaf than Beethoven. The only time I could hear a pin drop was in a bowling alley. During the years that followed, years of being at ground zero of many a thundering band, I was damn sure to always wear earplugs. (Yes, kids, a blatant plug for earplugs.)

So— for two hours on that mind-blowing night, as the stage slowly turned like a psychedelic merry-go-round, I got to see Jimi's point of view. It impacted me in such a way, that within the year I would pack up and move to California to become, of all things, a rock impresario. Even named my concert production company what Jimi had suggested: Heaven Research.

But I digress.

I took it all in. All those many thousands of bug-eyed, slack-jawed, smoke-veiled faces getting high as Jimi took them higher. And, not more than a couple feet from where I sat, my bell-bottom blue jeans dangling off the stage, Jimi dropped to his knees and set fire to his Voodoo Stratocaster. So, now, not only was my hearing in part gone, so were my eyelashes.

So, uh—have you ever been experienced? Well, I have.

Without the Q & A, the piece I submitted was mostly subjective and began . . .

> *Jimi Hendrix gets blown, does blow, blows 15,000 minds.*
> *(15,001, if you're counting this writer.)*

Oh, and as for my long-legged partner in crime, it turns out that even equipped with an expensive camera, wide-angle lens, the whole schmear—not to mention the extraordinary proximity to Jimi Hendrix—pretty Lolly somehow managed to take photos that were pretty lousy.

Fortunately, in the sack she was anything but.

* * *

1972

JAGGER'S BAR MITZVAH

My laidback friend Jon and I were sitting around his makeshift table (its base an oak wine barrel) smoking a doob and talking about the Rolling Stones coming to town. Somehow, we got off on this tangent about how cool it would be to see "The World's Greatest Rock and Roll Band" in a cozy nightclub setting—instead of having to brave the unruly crush of 10,000 maniacs crammed into an arena—with every table near the stage, and Jagger, like his song, is just a kiss away, kiss away, kiss away. And we started discussing, at first jokingly, how fucking amazing it would be to see the Stones at Bimbo's 365 Club, a swank Art Deco supper club in North Beach. Everyone would be dressed to the nines, some to the tens, and the tables dressed in red linen and, as a centerpiece, champagne on ice.

And then, I looked over at my friend, and he looked over at me, and we said in unison, *"Let's do it!"*

Not wanting to put the old cart before the horse, I thought it would be wise to first secure the venue before pitching the idea. So, I paid a visit to Agostino Giuntoli a.k.a. "Mr. Bimbo." He was a congenial gent with a pencil-thin mustache the color of cigar ash. He'd been running the legendary nightclub since 1931, presenting such top name acts as Rita Hayworth, Rodney Dangerfield, Marvin Gaye, Neil Diamond, Louis Prima and Keely Smith, and the like. What the famous Copacabana in the 1940s and '50s had been to New Yorkers, Bimbo's 365 Club had been to San Franciscans. But now here it was, at the start of the 1970s, and Bimbo's was available only on a rental basis for private events such as wedding receptions, first communion celebrations and the occasional bar mitzvah.

Mr. Bimbo—who, in his sixties, walked with a slight hunch— gave me a tour of the club. Judging by appearances, it was apparent the man was fond of sea life. And nudity. The mirrors were etched with curvaceous mermaids. In the lobby, was a white marble statue of a voluptuous nymph riding bareass on a ginormous goldfish, and he rhapsodized of a "naked girl in a fishbowl" that once had been the talk of the town. But, more importantly (the plethora of titties aside), I was certain the Stones would appreciate the club's large, curved stage draped with luxurious red velvet and its state-of-the-art sound and lighting. So, I reserved June 7th, the Stones' only San Francisco off day. On June 6th and 8th, they would be appearing at Winterland, performing two shows a night, to a combined capacity crowd of 21,600. Bimbo's, in comparison, was a mere 450-capacity, allowing those in attendance to truly "spend the night together" with the Rolling Stones. Sort of like having a close and personal tête-à-tête with Mick.

I told Mr. Bimbo we'd need maximum security. Obviously, he wanted to know who this world-famous big shot was that required his having to hire extra security, and I told him I was not yet at liberty to disclose.

He persisted. "A hint, at least!"

So, on my way out the door, to throw off the scent, I crooned, "Dooby dooby doooo—"

His eyes twinkled and, for a moment, I thought he might burst into a lively tarantella. He assured me his club would have more security than Fort Knox.

When he finally realizes it's Jagger up there on the stage and not Sinatra, he's going to be more than a tad ticked off. But I wasn't worried, because I was doing him a solid. When it got around town that the Rolling Stones had appeared at Bimbo's, the old nightspot would become the new hotspot. And Mr. Bimbo would be *dooby-dooby-dooing* all the way to the bank.

Being a cockeyed optimist, I'm also thinking that after the Stones play Bimbo's, I'll be able to book the Who. After all, the Who and the Stones had the same tour manager—Peter Rudge.

A couple days later, I ran the idea by him. I told Peter it would be a secret by-invitation-only affair. I described the club in lavish detail. Then added that instead of printing the invites on paper stock, we'd distribute small, rounded beach stones, on each would be hand-painted the famous "lips and tongue" Rolling Stones logo, known also as Hot Lips. To divert attention and further guard the show's secrecy, the Bimbo's marquee would simply read: BAR MITZVAH. (In fact, I was toying with the idea of including a calligraphed card with each hand-painted Hot Lips stone that would read: *You're cordially invited to the bar mitzvah of Michael Jaggerstone.*)

I tried making the pitch as enticing, yet brief, as I could—hopefully not squandering a single syllable—and waited for the band's tour manager's response. The silence felt like an eternity. Was my idea so preposterous that Peter had quietly hung up? Had I somehow come off like so many of the blowhards who approached him daily with some cockamamie idea? But, no, he was simply mulling things over. And, when he finally did comment—in an enthusiastic British clip that, to these Yankee Doodle ears, sounded much like the Duke of Edinburgh (which came as no surprise being that Peter represented rock and roll royalty)—he said it was a compelling proposition and sounded fantastically exciting, et cetera, and added that the group had been talking of doing something of this sort for some time.

But, then he asked why he should put his trust in me?

If ever was a time to toot my own horn, this was the time, and told him how I had fairly recently produced rock concerts at the Monterey Fairgrounds, the Fillmore West and the Marin Civic Auditorium—with the likes of Steve Miller, Canned Heat, Arthur Lee and Love, Spirit, Eric Burdon and War, Lee Michaels, Quicksilver Messenger Service, and Big Brother and the Holding Company, to name but a few.

Wanting to keep the conversation brief, I held back telling him that my concert promotion experience extended even beyond. But I'll fill you in.

About seven years earlier, when I arrived at boot camp in Cape May, New Jersey, the Drill Instructor, USCG Chief Petty Officer "Pudgy" Altman, asked the recruits in a barking, snarly voice, "Any college men?!" He said "college" with mock disdain, and I was the only mutt "brave" enough to raise a hand, and fortunately I did because he appointed me as yeoman of the newly formed Romeo Company. One of my responsibilities as the company's yeoman was to assign the enlisted men's duties, such as kitchen patrol and so forth. I never had to scrub a bulkhead or swab a deck, just made sure my bunk was squared-away and, on one occasion, stood midnight guard so one of the recruits could get some sorely needed shuteye. You might say I felt like that roguish character Phil Silvers portrayed in those old *Sgt. Bilko* reruns. When someone got cookies from home, it was shared with the yeoman in hopes of not getting KP duty.

Then, upon graduating from boot, and even though I was trained for shipboard duty, Pudgy—tough but tenderhearted—allowed me to stay on at the training center as head of public relations and also be their newspaper's cartoonist, which meant nightly vigils to nearby Wildwood, N.J., arriving back at the barracks no later than 0600 hours. Out on the town from revelry to reveille.

But, the point of all this is that, along with combat training, learning Morse Code and how to tie a clove hitch knot, I produced some pretty sweet USO rock shows as a side hustle.

But I digress.

Evidently, what I *did* tell Peter gained his trust because he started talking money. The Rolling Stones' asking price was fifty thousand—which, back in '72, was a lot of cheddar. I did the math (which I rarely did in high school) and it came out to my having to sell about four hundred of the hand-painted stones at $175 a pop.

"Fifty K's no problem," I said, and asked if we have a deal.

"Hang on," he said.

Apparently, there was a catch. A clause in Bill Graham's contract stated that the Rolling Stones were not permitted to advertise any other show within fifty miles, thirty days before or after their Winterland engagement. Peter asked if I could pull it off. I said I could. Though exactly *how* I'd pull it off was kept to myself.

My plan was unconventional. I would move the hand-painted stones the way a dealer moved kilos, and I intended to recruit several trustworthy dealers to be my sales force. This was at a time when practically everybody and their Uncle Charlie dealt some contraband or another, at least in the Bay Area. Longhaired businessmen would casually move pounds of weed at a Grateful Dead show while dancing like no one was watching—except, perhaps, for that hippie-garbed narc whose shiny Florsheims were a dead giveaway.

One of the pot dealers I had met while producing concerts in Monterey. We'll call him Wyatt. He was about as stringy as his below-shoulders hair. His girlfriend—we'll call her Dawn—was extraordinarily stunning. Dark-eyes, olive skin, long slender legs. The night of the concert, rather than their having to drive all the way back to the Bay Area at an ungodly hour, and attempt it stoned, I invited them to spend the night at my home in Carmel—which, incidentally, was a mere block from the beach, on a street aptly named Casanova. In kind, the next morning Dawn invited me to crash at their home in Marin, whenever. And "whenever" came around about a month later when the rock concert biz went south and I headed north to San Francisco to seek work, taking along only two of my most prized possessions. Ben, an Afghan Hound, and my portfolio of award-winning ads—my ace in the hole.

When I showed up at their hillside house in Tam Valley, Wyatt had one of his legs in a cast and hopped around on crutches. He stayed mostly in his bedroom surrounded by stacks of comic books and, naturally, being a pot dealer, stayed high all day. When I asked how he broke his leg, he said it wasn't he that broke it, implying someone else did—the unfortunate consequences of dealing with the wrong type of citizen. Dawn told me later, however, that someone had laced a joint with angel dust and unbeknownst to Wyatt, he had taken "a big ol' hefty toke." It only took a second for him to lose his equilibrium and, "like the doper klutz he was," tumbled down a flight of stairs.

I had a job interview that afternoon with an ad agency and Dawn accompanied me into the city. Since the day we first met in Carmel we were hot for one another, so the very moment we entered an empty elevator—even before the doors slid shut—our mouths desperately lunged at each other. Little were we aware that another passenger had boarded just before the doors fully closed, and not till the elevator stopped and the doors slid open did Dawn and I come up for air. That's when we noticed the urbane gent, mid-sixties, with a full head of gray hair wearing a dark Givenchy double-breasted suit. He got off first and walked into the lobby like he owned the place, which he did.

"Good morning, Mr. Richardson," said a receptionist at the front desk.

"Good morning, Louisa," he said, and headed down the hall and into a corner office.

On the way over, Dawn and I had smoked a joint in the car, and judging from the receptionist's sniffy glances, we must've reeked of marijuana. Either that, or she didn't approve of someone bringing a dog into the agency. Especially for a job interview.

Moments later, she said, "Mr. Richardson will see you now, Mr. Heaven." And the way she put it, it couldn't have been soon enough.

Dawn, taking Ben's leash, gave me more than just a parting kiss. "Good luck," she said. And I made my way down the hall, past a workforce in absolute conformity with the company's conventional dress code, and entered a corner office. As offices go, this one was larger than most, and behind a desk only slightly smaller than a tugboat sat the President/CEO of one of The City's foremost ad agencies. "Rich" Richardson resembled Mr. Dithers—Dagwood Bumstead's boss in the old comic strip "Blondie"—but, unlike the cartoon character, he didn't look the least crotchety. He seemed quite amused, in fact, and mentioned how, at first, he had thought there were two ladies making out in the elevator—a dig at my shoulder-length hair—until he caught a glimpse of my mustache. He chuckled, then mentioned how he thought this longhaired fella in leather jeans, one hand gripping the ass of a gorgeous lass, the other clutching a large black portfolio—"the way a swashbuckler clasped his cutlass"—might be the hire his creative department was in dire need of, and how, if "this 'Captain Blood' fella was as good a copywriter as he was a lady's man, the job would be his." And then punctuated his statement with an impish wink, "Just so long as he did his gallivanting *off* premises." Having said that, Rich finally unzipped the portfolio, flipped though my work—chuckling as he did. "Well, by gum, I like it," he said, and hired me right then and there.

Afterwards, Dawn and I had a few drinks and, by the time we got back to Marin, we were in pretty high spirits. Wyatt was holed up in the bedroom. She went in and asked if he needed anything— milk and cookies, that sort of thing. He said, no thanks, gonna catch some z's. She turned off the light and shut the door behind her.

We downed a couple flutes of celebratory bubbly and she led me into the guest bedroom, which shared a wall with Wyatt's bedroom.

"He's good 'n zonked," she said, "and when he is, usually sleeps right through the night."

After she placed a bowl of water on the floor for Ben, she came over and whispered, "We gonna keep on celebrating?"

"Uhm, you wouldn't happen to have an elevator in the house, would you?"

The idea of our getting it on with the boyfriend in the next room gave me momentary pause, emphasis on "momentary" because the celebration continued. Consumed by our passion, neither of us thought to close the door.

Our clothes in a pile on the floor (and atop a lampshade), her smooth bare legs lifted toward the ceiling, I ate her out the way one imagines Caligula hungrily gorging on the sweet flesh of a juicy peach. My tongue—twirling, flicking and plunging—performed acrobatic feats it never thought possible. She shuddered and squirmed, gasped and moaned, and right when she was about to climax (my chin soaked from "Caligula's peach"), from behind came the sound of a throat clearing. We froze, resembling an erotic Rodin. I looked behind me and there, standing in the doorway was Wyatt—crutches and nothing else.

Surprisingly, he didn't yell or club me with a crutch. Instead, he told Dawn in a calm voice to go into their bedroom, please. He waited until she picked up her clothes and padded out of the room. Then—not angrily, but noticeably disenchanted—he said, "You gotta leave in the morning, brother. Okay?"

"Okay," I said, feeling like a lump of shit, yet felt grateful he hadn't cast me out into the night. *Wow, you can take the boy out of the Summer of Love, but can't take the Summer of Love out of the boy!*

Our tails between our legs—mine metaphorically—Ben and I left at the crack of dawn. And, sadly, I would forever miss the crack of Dawn.

A year or so passed, when one afternoon in Sausalito I bumped into Wyatt and, crazy as it may seem, we were both delighted to see one another. We sat on a bench overlooking the bay and passed a joint back and forth. I apologized for going down on his girlfriend, and he smiled, good-naturedly, and said, "It's okay, brother, can't blame you one bit. Besides, she confessed how much she dug you."

"And I her."

I asked how she was, and he said she moved back to Texas.

"Oh, damn," I said. "I would've liked to have picked up where we had left off, before we were so rudely interrupted by her boyfriend."

He laughed, and why not? The weed was sublime. And by the time we finished off the joint, we were chums once more.

The point of all this is that Wyatt was an example of the upstanding nature of the dealers I would cherry-pick to move a quantity of the hand-painted stones.

But I digress.

My phone call with Peter Rudge, the Rolling Stone's tour manager, concluded on a cheery note. "Going to be fucking fun," he said, or words to that effect.

And, a day later came word that it was a go!

So, now that I had booked the Stones, it was time to gather the stones. Muir Beach had plenty that were polished and smoothed from the sand, wind, and wave action of the Pacific—flat, round and jagged little stones that, with the stroke of an artist's brush and some acrylic paint, would become "Jagger'd" little stones.

As I lugged a half-filled burlap sack of smooth beach pebbles, reality sank in. Had I, as the expression goes, bitten off more than I could chew? Or hand-paint? After all, without the persuasive power of conventional advertising, would I be able to sell enough stones to come up with the fifty large? It was a far greater weight upon my shoulders than a bag of beach pebbles. When I asked Jon, my laidback pal, what specific tasks he was taking on, he leaned back against his "Racing Green" Karmann Ghia ragtop, and, in his usual blasé manner, replied, "Gonna run out and buy a black velvet suit for the occasion."

But, as it turned out, before he could run out and buy the suit, or I could get more than a *few* stones painted, let alone distributed, a telegram arrived, and—poof! Just like that, the Stones were, all a sudden, a no-go.

Had Bill Graham given it the ol' kibosh?

Had the band been given some sort of ultimatum? Like, "do that *fakakta* Bimbo's gig and forget doing any more Bill Graham gigs!"

But, au contraire. When I asked Graham's "right hand man" Jerry Pompili—someone who knew the great rock impresario probably as well as anyone—he laughed.

"Bill didn't kill it," he said. "Hell, he loves stuff like that. Would've probably gone to that show, sat at a ringside table and had himself a grand ol' fuckin' time."

And so, it would remain a mystery for years.

Meantime, I put the incident behind me and directed my creative juices elsewhere. And like the old adage of one door closing and another one opening, what walked through the proverbial door turned out to be "The Greatest Fucking Rock Show on Earth."

The Tubes were introduced to me by the exotically beautiful Re Styles.

Re had made quite the worldwide splash when she appeared in *Penthouse, Playboy* and *Oui*—the triple crown of titty magazines— in the same month! A feat (and teat) unprecedented. She had also costarred in Alejandro Jodorowsky's surrealistic masterpiece The Holy Mountain. (On a related note, Re gave me a silver bracelet given to her by Jodorowsky that I brought to a jeweler to have the clasp fixed, and when I returned the next day, the clerk—a cinephile with a thievish nature—was gone, and so was the cherished bracelet.)

Me and Re.
Polaroid: Prairie Prince

Posing with bracelet Jodorowsky gave Re, who, in turn, gave me, shortly before it was snatched.
Photo: Mikel Covey

Earlier that year, Re married Alan Styles, the Pink Floyd roadie at City Hall. I was best man. A few months later, after an amicable parting of the ways, Re and her pup Luna (half Afghan, half Dane) moved in with me and my two Afghan Hounds, Ben and Sally. Soon after, she started seeing the drummer of an up-and-coming band called the Tubes and announced she would be joining them as a dancer and vocalist. (There was very little Re couldn't do.) She showed the Tubes my—by now notorious—"Sperm Whale Is Coming" poster and the band was anxious to meet me and do some brain-picking.

The Tubes were scheduled to open at Bill Graham's Winterland for Todd Rundgren and were looking for a kickass idea to get concertgoers there early, so as not to miss the opening act. I was made aware that drummer Prairie Prince and synthesizer keyboardist Michael Cotten were outstanding artists, and it was top of mind when, one day driving past Winterland, I noticed a vacant thirty-foot billboard on the side of the building. A blank canvas, so to speak. So, I immediately got Bill Graham on the phone and asked if the Tubes could paint something on it.

"Go right ahead," Bill said. "Knock yourselves out."

And, oh man, did we ever.

Working through the night and using primarily an airbrush

gun, Prairie and Mike painted lead singer Fee Waybill in a leather bondage mask, holding open a trench coat (in the classic flasher pose) revealing a BDSM leather outfit. The message read simply: The Tubes Open Winterland . . . 8:00 May 17-18. Thereby beginning my long and intimate association with those White Punks On Dope.

But what does all this have to do with Mick and the boys?

Flash forward four years.

The Tubes are now in full stride, blowing minds right and left, night after night as resident performers at The Boarding House, a historic music and comedy venue on San Francisco's Bush Street.

Art: Prairie Prince and Michael Cotten ·
Photo: Mikel Covey · Concept: Edwin Heaven ·

I had become the band's "Ambassador of Ballyhoo," "Prime Minister of Propaganda" and, not to be taken lightly, a proud member of its stellar cast—particularly on their grand finale "White Punks On Dope." I would prance out on stage, performing various oddball stunts—for example, I would hold a can of Coke in each hand and simultaneously crush them against my forehead (the cans being empty, of course, as was my head)—and then dance around with The Tubettes. On occasions, I also sang some backup: *white punks on dope, white punks on dope, white punks on dope*, ad nauseam. As it happens, I was also "Emissary of Wackadoo" and a frequent challenge was finding wacky ways of transporting Quay Lewd onto the stage. For example, at one particular Winterland show, Quay was carted out on a tonjon by a half-dozen six-foot-tall Amazon women dressed in skimpy animal skins. And at the Paramount Theater in Oakland, a half dozen body builders—their muscular pecs, biceps and quadriceps greased and glistening—carried him onto the stage as if he was no heavier than the feathered boa—which he wore, along with a shaggy blonde wig and two-foot-high platform shoes (which made the six-foot tall Waybill appear eight feet tall).

But one of my pet contributions was the time I was asked by Francis Ford Coppola's *City* magazine to write a piece on the Tubes. And when the band invited me to write it right there on stage (from a Tubes-eye view) I didn't bat an eyelash. (Although, I do admit, I did seem to develop a twitch in my left nostril by the time it was all over.)

An equipment-man with KILL in white letters plastered on his black T-shirt led me by a sweaty elbow to the middle of the stage, where a typewriter awaited me. There I sat, between the bass player and the Moog synthesizer, petrified that I might accidently touch one of the millions of electrical wires covering the stage and get fried like a zucchini. (Thank goodness they gave me an acoustic Royal!)

Out there, somewhere beyond the green-tangerine haze, a sellout crowd chanted: "White punks on dope! White punks on dope!" Little did I know at the time that also in the crowd chanting along with everyone else was none other than Mick Jagger—whom we will come to snortly. I mean, shortly.

Gradually the feeling returned to my fingertips, and I began writing the magazine piece, the keys getting stuck on every other word. But it didn't matter, I was right smack dab in the middle of the Tubes' classic "White Punks on Dope" finale and my seat was the best in the house. An explosive flash transformed the entire stage into an erotic, raunchy Cecil B. De Milligram production. A phantasmagoria of Ed Sullivan reruns. A Norman Rockwell wet dream. What seemed like a cast of thousands drifted, tumbled, danced, and somersaulted in wall-to-wall fog—after all, we were a San Francisco band. It was great entertainment, but not the family kind. A ballerina was gang-raped by Leo Gorcey and The Disco Boys. Leila the Snake (the inimitable Jane Dornacker) turned her cleavage into the San Andreas fault, nine-point-sex on the Richter scale. Dizzy Heights (a name I had the distinction of bestowing) did everything a big top trapeze aerialist could do and did it topless. Quay Lewd (Fee Waybill's alter ego), as always, sported a foot-long rubber dildo inside his stretch silver lamé tights. And Miss Tammy Van Upp belly danced, while her undulating python—longer than Wilt the Stilt—twisted around her bare torso and other parts.

Edwin Heaven playing a typewriter á la Jimi Hendrix.

(On a side note, Tammy would on occasion spend the night, and before bedding down we'd stack a tower of heavy objects like dictionaries, bricks, and barbell weights on top of the straw basket in which her seven-foot-two snake slept, so it wouldn't slither out during the night and mistake one of my Afghans as a midnight snack. Yes, I slept lightly.)

Oh, and yes, I played the typewriter with my teeth.

After the show, I apologized to the band for typing a little off key and fought my way through a mess of groupies trying to get a cheap feel of my now famous fingertips. That's when I noticed, heading toward me, Jerry Pompili with Mick Jagger and Annie Leibovitz in tow.

Straightaway, Jerry said, "The Tubes just blew Mick's mind."

"What's left of it," Mick said, grinning behind Ray Ban aviators. "Would love to meet the lads." He was practically starstruck. This was a Jagger I had not seen before—not in concert, not in interviews or on film—and it was positively charming.

"I'll see what I can do, Mick," I said, trying to keep a straight face. And added, as I escorted them backstage, "It's Sputnik Spooner's birthday, so let's surprise him!"

The moment we entered the greenroom, I made a beeline to the birthday boy, Mick close behind and doing his best to go unnoticed.

"Sputnik," I said, "I brought you a little something for your birthday."

And, right on cue, Mick leaped out from behind me.

"Happy fookin' birthday, Sputnik!"

Annie took some photos—one of Fee and Mick wound up in the pages of Rolling Stone magazine.

I took Mick around and introduced various members of the troupe. That's when he noticed the Tubes' drummer Prairie Prince cooling off by an open window, a sweat-soaked towel wrapped around his neck.

"Hey, I know you!" said Mick in his faux-Cockney accent. "You're Prairie Prince!"

Prairie—a double for Robert Mitchum, and just as cool—replied, "And I know you! You're Mick Jagger!"

Turns out, Prairie Prince had played on a Nicky Hopkins album along with Mick Jagger and bandmates Mick Taylor and Ron Wood—not to mention Beatle George Harrison. (Not only was Prairie one of the world's best drummers, he was also one of its least boastful.)

Afterwards, we met up at The Orphanage. Once a Playboy Club, it was now a rock and roll hotspot. Its owner was most accommodating and had roped off a large round table. Holding court as if it were the famed Algonquin roundtable were the Jaggers, Bianca looking even more striking in person. Slumped to her right was Ronnie Wood, already drunk as a lord. I was seated to Mick's left. He turned to me and asked if I had any "humps." I hadn't the foggiest what that was, so he put two fingers to his pillowy lips and exhaled an imaginary puff of smoke.

"Ohh," I said. "Camels!"

"Yeh, wha'ja *think* I meant? Fookin' Quasimodos?"

Turned out to be Mick's lucky night, because Re smoked the same brand, and they went through that pack in no time.

Bianca and I had a heavy discussion about Pop Art (Warhol) as opposed to Modernism (O'Keeffe). After much quaffing—"Woody" leading the pack—we all somehow ended up at a party in the East Bay, where, without delay, we were glad-handed by a lanky chap sporting a scaled-down, less-elaborate Daliesque mustache. This was Danny Lee, the obsequious shutterbug, who had found another calling and tapped his nose, silently trumpeting that he was the man with the goods. Mick said something about being knackered and Danny astutely opened a door and with a grandiose gesture invited us all inside. "Step into my office, Mr. Jagger," he said, twirling the mustache.

It was a walk-in closet and, once inside, I said to Mick, "Who says you don't always get what you want?"

It was close quarters, but Annie still managed to fire off some shots, although careful not to include within the camera's view any of us—particularly Mick—toot-toot-tooting. No easy task, believe you me. Not even for The Great Leibovitz.

Taking advantage of the proximity, I reminded Mick of the time in '72 when I approached the Rolling Stones to do a secret show at Bimbo's 365 Club.

"That was you?"

I did a mock bow. Then careful not to step on any toes, figuratively and literally, I inquired as to why it didn't come about.

He shrugged. "Mate, I just sing and dance. That's management's department. But I faintly recall doing two shows a night and the band, being knackered, needed the off day."

Mick paused as Danny steered a tittle of toot beneath his snoot. Maybe Danny had his nose, but I still had his ear—although not completely, what with everyone crammed into a tight space, blitzed on coke, and jabbering all at once. But, I did manage to tell him how I had planned to put on the Bimbo's marquee, as a diversion, just the words BAR MITZVAH. Mick chuckled. At least I think it was a chuckle. Could've been a snuffle, so I wisely withheld telling him my other idea about them coming out on stage wearing snazzy yarmulkes. Mick would've looked at me as if I'd gone barmy, and surely would've drawn the line at having to wear a skullcap—snazzy or not. Our little tête-à-tête was cut short again as another dollop of Danny's bodacious blow appeared—to which we were all more than obliging.

The four of us then tumbled out of that closet like the Marx Brothers.

Across the room, I spotted someone I knew—and wanted to know better.

"Cheerio," I said to Mick.

"Porridge," he said to me, and we laughed.

She and I ended up catching a ride back to my North Beach digs, and, as improbable as it might seem, the night got even better.

But, hey—I digress.

Fee and me.
Photo by Danny Lee.

* * *

EDWIN HEAVEN

1972

THE PANAMANIAN REDHEAD

I was racing to catch a ferry when my housemate Ben decided at this inopportune moment to stop and water a rhododendron. He probably figured the plant needed a good dousing because by the time he lowered his leg, the ferry had proceeded without us. Gave us the slip, so to speak. So when a VW van heading toward the bridge approached, I instinctively stuck out a thumb. The van grinded to a halt and we hopped in.

Behind the wheel was a redhead with the greenest eyes this side of Emerald City. She was a damn pretty little thing with milk-white skin and a sprinkling of freckles. A Renoir, I thought—or perhaps a "New Age" Botticelli. She stroked Ben's long muzzle and I nearly barked out of sheer envy. She spoke as she stroked and mentioned how much she was missing her dog. Sage, his name was. Reason I remember, I had made some lame remark about her maybe adopting two more dogs and naming one Parsley and the other Thyme.

"Where can I drop the two of you off?" she asked.

I told her anywhere near Van Ness Avenue. I also told her I had a freshly rolled spliff.

"Panamanian Red," I said.

She pushed in the lighter and when it was orange hot, handed it to me. I lit the doob, taking only a tiny toke. I learned from recent experience how good this shit was and didn't take very much to get you good and fucked up. I passed it over and the toke she took was not the least tiny. She pulled on it till the ember glowed like a horny firefly, did a double hit, held it in for a prolonged period—no neophyte she—then exhaled a long, wispy cloud.

She tried to contain a cough but to no avail. Then laughed and coughed some more.

"Righteous dope," she said, laughing and coughing. "What didja say it was?"

"Panamanian . . . *Redhead.*"

She laughed again, which set in motion another round of coughing. Then, to further compound matters, she hiccupped. Here she was, practically simultaneously, coughing, hiccupping, and laughing. Somehow, by the grace of God, she managed to keep the vehicle on the road. Ben placed a big paw on her lap, perhaps out of canine concern. Either that, or he was on the make. As was I.

While all this physiological madness was going on, I made believe I was calling Ed Sullivan on a rotary phone. (When I get stoned, I get goofy.)

"Hello, Ed? I said into the imaginary phone. "Oh boy, have I an act for you!" I imitated one of them old-timey theatrical agents. "She coughs! She laughs! She hiccups! And she can do it all at once! And," I said, giving her a sideways glance, "she's super easy on the retinas!" I placed a hand over the imaginary mouthpiece, and stage whispered, "Ed Sullivan!" Then once again into the pretend phone added, "What's the name of her act you ask? It's The Panamanian Redhead!"

"And tell him," she said, playing along, "I can do all that while standing on my head reciting existential poetry!" She took another hefty toke and, this time thank goodness, she neither coughed nor hiccupped, and had little trouble staying on the road. "You can also tell Ed Sullivan I think he's a dick."

I laughed and, into the invisible phone, said, "She's also quite funny!" I pantomimed slamming the handset into the telephone cradle, which got a laugh.

"This is superb fucking weed," she said, trying to hold it in while at the same time talk, which, obviously, was another of her many talents. "And I ought to know . . . I was born in a town called Weed."

She then asked if I was a dealer.

No," I said. "I write." And asked what she did.

She was in between things, she said. Had owned a boutique in Los Angeles where Sharon Tate had shopped from time to time.

Then her mood suddenly changed, and she let drop that she recently had become a widow.

I didn't know what to say. After all, I was just some random hitchhiker. A stranger. So, hoping to keep things light and copacetic, I didn't say anything. Just a murmured "Sorry."

She turned on the radio, perhaps to fill an awkward silence, and, of all songs, the station was playing Stephen Stills' "Love the One You're With," the gist of which is: If you can't be with the one you love, honey, love the one you're with.

How very, very weird, I thought. I mean, what were the odds?

I've always had a *thing* for redheads. The first girl I ever kissed was a redhead. We weren't much older than five. It was in the backseat of my father's Buick. Up there in the front bench seat, my dad and the man whose daughter I was kissing thought it was quite a cute sight and egged us on. "Kiss her like Robin Hood kissed Maid

Marian," my dad joked. And so, I did. Or at least how I imagined a noble thief like Robin would. And I've had, like I said, a thing for redheads ever since.

And here I was with quite possibly the prettiest redhead this side of Sherwood Forest.

Anyway, time flew, blah blah blah, and here we were, already on Van Ness Avenue. I didn't recall our even crossing the bridge.

She pulled the van over and I thanked her for the lift. She thanked me for the buzz. As I opened the door to step out, she leaned forward as if to give me a kiss, but, instead, planted one on Ben's Cyranoesque snout.

Why don't you two lovebirds get a room? My room!

She must've had extrasensory perception, or picked up on my vibe, because she mentioned she was meeting friends at the No Name Bar like around nine and would we like to join her?

Absofuckinglutely. Although, what I said was, "I'd love to. And, speaking of 'no name,' mine's Edwin. My long-muzzled friend is Ben, short for Benji Baba. And yours?"

"Pam," she said, with a big toothy grin, "The Panamanian Redhead."

*   *   *

The No Name was a popular watering hole in Sausalito, even though very few Sausalitans were drinking water. The place was awash with the usual oddballs: poets, rockers, and waterfront pirates. As usual, a serious game of chess was in progress. The big open window at the front of the bar looked out upon a pair of large concrete elephants, but if you craned your neck and looked down at the sidewalk, you'd also see a tall, slim, silky brindled Afghan Hound hitched outside the saloon like a pony.

There was a highly recognizable fellow with a shaved head and black beard standing over by the bar. Next to him was a free-spirited brunette of notorious reputation known occasionally to wear a nun's habit at local council meetings—although, tonight, the haute couture was a sleeveless t-shirt displaying sinewy arms. This, of course, was the erstwhile prostitute and sex-worker activist Margo St. James. And you'd be on the money if you guessed that the bald, bearded fellow was the internationally famous songwriter, poet and *Playboy* magazine cartoonist Shel Silverstein.

"How's the cloud car?" Shel asked.

"Like Proud Mary," I replied, "she keeps on burnin'."

He did a few do-do-do-do-do's like he was singing backup for Tina Turner, and we exchanged low fives, rebop-style. I had recently given Shel a lift from his houseboat, moored at Gate 5, into downtown Sausalito, and he especially dug my old VW Bug. I had commissioned an artist by the name of Christos to paint the body a sky blue with pink puffy clouds. A paint job, I might add, that cost more than the car. Word was that when crossing the Golden Gate Bridge, particularly during the twilit hours when the sky was fluffed with pinkish clouds, the "art car" became camouflaged and seemed to disappear into thin air.

"I'm looking for a pretty redhead," I said.

"Hell, who isn't?" Shel said.

"I can fix you both up, if you want," Margo said.

"Another time, perhaps," I said, more as a courtesy.

I tapped on the window to get Ben's attention, let him know I was nearby. He sat up, his tail, curled like a question mark, moved quickly from left to right.

"Afghans remind me of those Popeye creatures," Shel said. "Goons, that's what they're called."

"Mind keeping an eye on the 'goon,'" I said, "while I have a quick look-around?"

"'I ain't no tailor, but I know what suits me,'" he said, citing Popeye. "But hurry back. Never know when Uncle Shelby has to make a mad dash for the head."

"Is that a dog barking?" Margo asked, pricking an ear.

Shel snorted. "Those are *seals*, Margo, dear."

From across the room, somebody called out my name. It was the artist Larry Moyer a.k.a. King of the Waterfront, who currently had a role in Robert Downey's latest oddball comedy *Greaser's Palace*. I crossed the room to his table.

"I had a hunch you'd be here," I said. "Where there's a Silverstein, you'll usually find a Moyer."

"Like Frick and Frack," said the one-time matinee idol seated across from Moyer. Sterling Hayden was still big in Hollywood—earlier that year he played the corrupt police captain in Francis Ford Coppola's *The Godfather*—but here at the ol' No Name Bar, he was just another rugged seafarer and soused author.

"Like you 'n liquor," countered Moyer.

"Liquor and me," said Hayden, "we're in a stable relationship."

Hayden knew a thing or two about relationships, stable or otherwise. At last count, he'd been married five times, although three of the marriages were to the same woman, actress Madeleine Carroll. Paramount Pictures had called her "The Beautiful Blond Brit Goddess" to go hand-in-hand with "The Beautiful Blond Viking God," which was what the studio had called her six-foot-five handsome husband Hayden.

I took in the room, saw nothing but blondes and brunettes, and asked the fellas if they'd seen a pretty redhead.

"Is that the title of some movie?" asked Hayden.

"In the back, I saw a ginger schmoozin' 'n boozin' with Brautigan 'n Carpenter," said Moyer. "So I were you, I'd make hay."

So, make hay I did.

And there she was out back, in the open patio with the overhead greenery, looking radiant and rosy, holding court with two celebrated men of letters. One was Don Carpenter, author of the extraordinary first novel *Hard Rain Falling*, the other was the poet Richard Brautigan, who caught the zeitgeist of the 1960s with *Trout Fishing in America*.

Don and I had become instant chums one afternoon when a skiff we were on stalled a good ways from shore. The boat belonged to Stephen Frisch, a mutual friend and consummate photographer I had worked with on several shoots. Don told me not to worry, Steve could fix just about anything. So, while he tinkered with the motor and the boat drifted further from shore, Don and I, a couple landlubbers, just sat there smoking weed, drinking beer, exchanging horrific tales of Hollywood and, mainly, just chewing the fat. We knew we were in a pickle, but it didn't stop us from laughing our fool heads off. We were like a couple Oliver Hardys to Stephen Frisch's Stan Laurel, if you get the picture. "Here's another fine mess you've gotten us into, Stanley," we said to Steve. But as the bridge passed overhead and the boat drifted closer to the mouth of the Pacific, we feared we might wind up like ol' Robinson Crusoe and his man Friday.

"You be Friday," Don said. "I look nothing like Jack Webb." Don had a round merry face with the kindest eyes and a high receding hairline. Jack Webb, of course, being the deadpan actor with a flattop who played Sergeant Friday on the old cop show *Dragnet*.

"Dum de-DUM-DUM!" I sang, mimicking the show's ominous theme.

Fortunately, there was no need for a Coast Guard rescue. By the time Steve got the engine roaring, we were roaring drunk. Nonetheless, we cracked open celebratory beers.

"Here's to all the Frisches in the sea," Don said, toasting our heroic skipper.

"And here's to happy endings," I said, toasting the roaring engine.

"There are no happy endings," Don said, with his usual calm demeanor, "outside of Hollywood movies and massage parlors." Somehow, he managed to say this without a shred of morose, so we all laughed.

I had met Richard Brautigan around the same time. It was

at The Trident, the legendary restaurant perched on the Sausalito waterfront, where the waitresses sported nose rings, see-through blouses and friendly smiles that gave one the impression they were waiting to go home with you, and they would often find on the table, along with the usual gratuity, a long fat line of coke.

I was over by the bar sipping a Tequila Sunrise, The Trident's signature drink, when I noticed a tall, lanky dude wearing a big broad-brimmed hat standing beside me and, right away, wished I had been drinking something less frou-frou, like a whiskey neat. He looked like a cross between Mark Twain and a hippie Gary Cooper. He threw back a shot, quaffed a pint of Anchor Steam, then with an inky index finger gracefully flicked the creamy foam from his walrus mustache and, out of the fucking blue, said, "Here it is barely September and already there's an inch of snow in Texas." Sounded like one of his succinct, surreal poems. (The Brautigan poem that came to mind was the one that went: *At 1:03 in the morning a fart/ smells like a marriage between/ an avocado and a fish head.*) Was it possible the man was hip to climate change decades before it became in vogue? Or was he simply a few sheets to the wind and looking to make some pleasant banter.

Sadly, a decade later, he would put a bullet through his head.

Sadder still, eleven years after Richard, Don would do the same.

But I digress.

I detected, behind Richard's wire-rimmed granny glasses, a conspiratorial glint as he said to Pam, "Is this the guy from Panama?" And they all laughed.

I did, too. Not just because it was funny but also because I was glad she had been talking about me.

Pam, unaware that her friends were also my friends, introduced me as the writer she had "picked up." This also got a collective chuckle.

"Edwin Heaven writes like hell!" Don smiled warmly. Our being adrift on the bay and jabbering all day, there was little he didn't know about me, and vice versa, including the catchphrase I had started using to drum up writing gigs.

"What is it you write?" Richard asked.

I mentioned my having just wrapped an anti-war TV spot and how I had the good fortune to have as my DP the Oscar-winning cinematographer Haskell Wexler, blah blah blah.

Pam seemed impressed and wanted details. What it was about, how did it go, and so forth. I glanced over at Don and like a third base coach he gave me the swing away sign, which was just a simple nod, a *go for it, kid*, so to speak, so I swung for the fences.

"It opens with a medium shot," I heard myself saying,

unconsciously framing the shot with director's hands and wishing I hadn't. "He's a hard-on in a business suit. Maybe a former leatherneck who perhaps invested a bundle in Dow Chemical, those wonderful folks who brought you napalm, someone you'd imagine played golf with Tricky Dick. Wexler's camera pushes in slowly and keeps pushing until, at the end, we see an extreme close-up. The actor, his face partially in shadow, looks directly at us and, in a low menacing growl, says, 'I am War. Help me kill. All you have to do is do nothing. Don't protest. Don't write your congressman. In fact, you can do me a favor. Don't even *think* of me. I am War. Help me . . . *kill.*'"

Don applauded. "Bravo!"

"Reverse psychology," said Pam. "I like. Who'd you cast in the role?"

"A complete unknown," I said. "Anthony Quinn wanted to do it, so did Henry Fonda, but we didn't want a famous face because the guy says, 'I am War.' We didn't want the folks at home yelling at their TV sets, 'The hell you are! You're Anthony Fuckin' Quinn!'"

Richard jotted something on a cocktail napkin and handed it to me.

12-16, it read.

Was it something to do with Nam? Demarcation lines, maybe? I was at a loss.

"It's a screenwriter's formula for success," he explained. "Twelve-to-sixteen-year-olds, that's who Hollywood makes movies for."

To this day, I don't know whether he was serious or just pulling my leg, but I taped that napkin on the wall above my typewriter and heeded his advice, nonetheless. And, not too many years later, it paid off—led to my writing a script for Stan Lee that would become the first film in the Marvel Cinematic Universe.

But that's another story.

Richard drained his glass. "And here's another little Hollywood tip. Let's say you're at Dan Tana's or Musso & Frank's and you run into some big studio fat cat and he asks what you're working on, just say—" And here he paused, looked over at Don with a grin.

And Don picked up right where Richard left off. "Just say you're working on several projects in various stages of development." He had completed Richard's sentence like they were a couple comedians, and this was just one of their many running gags.

Pam placed a hand on my arm. "Did you bring Benji Baba?"

"He's out front," I said. And with a wink, "Waiting for you."

This did the trick, I guess, because she stood up, gave both Don and Richard a peck on the cheek, took my hand and led the way to the front of the bar.

First thing I did when we got there was to thank Shel for

looking after Ben.

"Ben?" he said, straight-faced. "Ben who?"

I dashed over to the window and thanked my lucky stars he was still there, reposed like The Great Sphinx of Giza. Ben had not been dognapped and I heaved a sigh of relief.

Shel chuckled. He had deked me.

Ben, seeing me standing there at the window, let out a joyful woof.

"Now that's a seal!" said Margo.

"No, Margo," said Shel. "*That's* a dog."

"Well, hell, Shel," she said, "I wish you'd make up your frickin' mind."

In the meantime, Pam had grabbed two seats at the bar by the window, all the better to keep an eye on Ben. "If not for that dog of yours," she said, "I doubt I would've stopped to pick you up." Then, leaning in real close, her lips brushing my ear—she smelled of honeysuckle and seashells—said, matter-of-factly, "Wanna split a lude, dude?"

"Do the Beatles do it in the road?"

"Just John," she said, breaking a Quaalude in two and slipping me half.

The night was full of promise, all seemed to be going

swimmingly—but then some shitfaced Romeo got right up behind her and, low and raspy, warbled into her ear, "C'mon, baby, light my fie-ya."

Jesus, that's gotta be the worst pick up line of all time.

Evidently, she thought so, too, because she ignored him the way you would some pesky moth flitting about. Having picked up on her complete indifference, Moth Man fluttered off.

The moment he was gone, she turned to me, face drawn.

"Let's go hang with Benji Baba," she said.

My long-muzzled best friend, Ben.

She was only in town for a week or so, staying just up the hill from the No Name as a houseguest of Papa John Creach, the renowned blues violinist, who was away on tour with the Jefferson

Airplane. Or was it Hot Tuna? She wasn't sure.

On the way up the hill we smoked "The Redhead," as we now called it. A narrow pathway of night blooming jasmine led to a steep stairway of at least a hundred wooden steps through the wooded hillside. Ben loped up the stairs like a deer, stopping here and there, of course, to water a tree, a plant, a hydrant. Obviously, he wasn't as eager as I to reach our destination. As far as Ben was concerned, whatever he lifted a leg on became his personal property. By all accounts, he owned about half of Sausalito, not to mention my entire heart. And, from the look on Pam's face, it wouldn't be long before he owned a piece of hers, too. If lucky, maybe I would, also.

The Quaalude kicked in the moment we stepped inside the house and everything just felt right, and when it's right . . . well, it's *right*. You can feel it in your bones. (Or, in my case, bone.) Our mouths came together, and it wouldn't be long before we would, too.

We fucked till blue in the face. Or, in Pam's case, a ravishing reddish glow.

I was still catching my breath when she reached up and grabbed some sheets of paper off the nightstand and stood up on the bed, rocking slightly. Ben, who had been curled up at the foot dreaming of green pastures and Milk-Bones, sat up as if a treat was forthcoming. It was a treat, all right, but not the Milk-Bone kind. There Pam stood, in the altogether, a pale, slender leg on each side of me, her neatly trimmed muff—still moist from our lovemaking—at just about eyelevel and tongue-distance. As I mentioned, she was petite. And, yes, she was also a genuine redhead.

"Since you're a writer, and so was my husband, would you like me to read some of his poetry?"

I nodded yes, of course, having the best seat in the house. As she read, I could see that the words, written in a cursive, were on lined ledger paper, the bookkeeping kind, and wondered if her late husband had been an accountant. But whatever he'd done for a living, his poetry was brilliant, rhythmic, and totally bizarre. Stuff like shaking dreams from hair, and golden copulations, and something about a cunt gripping like a warm friendly hand. Then came a verse that sounded vaguely familiar, and I'm thinking, *This guy ... maybe he's a plagiarist?* But, of course, that's not something you'd rightly tell a widow. So, with rapt attention I listened, ears pricked, as she read on. But then she came to a stanza that was more than just vaguely familiar. Something about faces, coming out of the rain.

And then, holy fuck! It registered.

"Your husband ... was he Jim Morrison?" I said this not as coolly as I would've liked.

She looked genuinely surprised. "You didn't know?"

"No," I said. "But, if I had, I most likely would've been intimidated."

But no, wait. That wasn't true. For at that very moment, I remembered some girl back in Philly who had taken me back to her place, no shrinking violet she, and there on the wall above her bed was a giant poster of Jim Morrison. (You probably know the one: bare-chest, leather pants, an aura of wavy locks.) And this girl, abandoning all further pretense, said, "Fuck me like Jim Morrison!" Whatever the fuck that might entail, I had no idea, but was certainly game—*hello, I love you, let me jump in your game*—and, her wish being my command, I fucked her the way I imagined Morrison might've, which was six ways from Sunday, etc&etc., and my imagination that night, needless to say, was somewhere along the lines of a D.H. Lawrence or, better still, a Charles Bukowski.

And now, here I was, in the sack with Pamela Courson. The Widow Morrison. Go figure.

And there she was, gazing down at me in a state of awe—which, apart from California, is my favorite state—then fell to her knees and took hold of my flaccid cock.

"Are you intimidated now?" she asked with that toothy grin.

"Not even a little bit," I said, rising to the occasion.

And off we rode, deep into the night. Like riders on the storm.

* * *

EDWIN HEAVEN

1976

MOON IN RONSTADT

I was standing at the corner of Broadway and Montgomery, one foot off the curb, about to cross, when this long black limo pulled up and, luckily, stopped a foot short of flattening my foot. I jumped back, but not far enough because when the rear door flew open, my knee got thwacked. I stumbled backward from the jolt just as a passenger stumbled out, roaring drunk, and closely trailed by not one but three ladies of the night, their hemlines well above the knees, their necklines plunged dramatically, the smell of their perfume assaulted my nostrils. Bent over as I was, rubbing a banged knee, all I glimpsed were long skinny legs and copious cleavage. They wore preposterously high stilettos and needed to lean over to kiss the john goodnight. Which was when I noticed it was Keith Moon, the Who's exalted drummer. Then, their ticket properly punched, the three escorts—who I'm fairly certain were the high-priced spread—stepped back into the stretch and off they went.

Moon zipped up his fly and spat whatever had lingered on the tip of his tongue. A pubic hair, perhaps—or maybe three. He peered around, getting his bearings, unsure whether he was in North Beach or Trafalgar Square. And that's when he noticed me, still bent over, still rubbing my kneecap.

"Hey, mate," he called, though he didn't need to, I was no more than an expectorated pubic hair away. "The City Disco . . . where the devil is it?"

I straightened up and pointed across the street. "It's the brick building with the big long line."

"Fuck big long lines," he said with a besotted grin, "unless they're laid out on a mirror."

We had a laugh. His sounded like drum strokes in triple meter.

"Sorry about the knee, mate," he said, and threw an arm around me. "Come along, I'll buy you a round."

We crossed the street—he teetered, I tottered—and with his arm slung over my shoulder, we must've looked like a couple drunken shipmates out on liberty. And in an instant, he was the center of attention. I offered my sunglasses, thinking he'd want to be less conspicuous, but he waved it off. He said he liked the recognition and, as if to prove a point, he walked up to the disco on his hands! The doorman parted the red velvet rope and Keith hand-walked inside.

Downstairs, we passed a small cabaret—I don't recall who was appearing that night (maybe Sylvester, maybe Grace Jones)—and headed upstairs to the largest dance floor in the Bay Area. A DJ sat high above in a booth made to look like a pulsating jukebox. We grabbed a couple stools at the bar in the back that had a panoramic view of the dance floor. Everybody was groovin' and movin' to The Hustle. Keith drummed on the surface of the bar, tapping along with Van McCoy and The Soul City Symphony. Even without the usual drum set—snare, bass, toms, cymbals, and whatnot—he was astonishing.

A bartender came over, a moustache with biceps.

"You're not bad, pal," he said to the most famous drummer in the world (aside from Ringo). Then to me, he asked, "Your friend in a band?"

"The Who," I said, barely audible above the ear-shattering speakers.

"The *what?*" he asked, cupping an ear.

"Not the What," Moon replied, "the Who." Then, as an aside, quipped, "Fuckin' Abbott and Costello, won't leave me the fuck alone."

I laughed, acquainted with the comedy duo's classic routine.

The bartender, meanwhile, looked blown away. "You're Keith Moon? Seriously?"

"I'm hardly ever serious," Keith said, enjoying the moment. "And hardly ever sober." Then, ordered two drinks. I was about to thank him when he asked me what I was drinking.

"Whatever you're having," I said. "But just one at a time for me, thank you."

Keith took out a roll and peeled off a couple twenties, but the bartender shook his head and said this round's on him, then bowed as if Keith was the Prince of Wales. He walked away to the other side of the bar to take an order and probably mutter to the customer that the great Keith Moon was in the house. Keith didn't mind at all. In fact, he would probably climb up to the DJ's booth, get on the mic and announce his royal presence himself. This was a bloke who liked to rock out with his cock out and was not averse to showing his wedding tackle in public.

Something or someone on the perimeter of the dance floor caught Keith's eye.

"Is that Linda Ronstadt?"

I looked over and, whoever she was, she was a dead ringer for Ronstadt.

"And she's makin' eyes at me," he said. "Or is it you?"

"Me and you," I said. "Or maybe she's just cockeyed."

"Would fancy meeting her, have a bit of a chat," he said. "Always pictured Linda singin' that song to me, but instead of sayin' 'different drum' she says, 'different *drummer*.'"

Those three escorts he was with not very long ago came to mind and I said, "I'm surprised you're not all fuckered out."

"Me? Fuckered out? Never!" (When he's not banging drums or random kneecaps, I'm thinking, he's banging primo poontang. Or is it *Moontang*?) "I'd be wipin' me sweat off with a towel after a show," he continued, "and they'd be lined up like lollipops in a sweet shop."

I don't think he was being boastful, he was simply stating a rock star fact. But, nonetheless, I kidded him about sounding a tad too much like the perverted child molesting babysitter he played in *Tommy*.

He sniggered like Uncle Ernie. Then he closed an eye as if to get a less blurry look at her. "That's Linda Ronstadt alright."

I looked over at her again and, as if she knew me, she smiled. I slid down from the stool, told him I'd be right back and to sit tight.

"I'm as tight as a tick on a fat man's bum," he said.

As I walked toward her, she swayed to the music. I was now close enough to make out her features. Eyes and hair brown—check. Cute turned up nose—check. Baby cheeks and bangs even longer than Keith Moon's—check, check. It was as if she had just stepped out of a Ronstadt album cover.

"Lin-da?" I asked, a twinge of uncertainty.

"Ha! So, you *do* remember me."

I thought it odd that I didn't recall ever having met Ronstadt.

"I was blond back then," she said, helping me to remember. "We met at the Trident. You chatted us up, me and my girlfriend, and then that guy from Blood, Sweat & Tears came over and we all wound up at his place. Remember?"

Oh, did I ever! David Clayton-Thomas, at first, came off like a really nice guy and was a genial host, especially generous with his blow—laid out some pretty fat lines—but then he fell into a dark mood and started pacing the room, angry about something or another and, all a sudden, he whipped out a gun, pointed it across the room at a framed photo no more than a couple feet from where the three of us sat. And bang! He put a bullet into the forehead of Al Kooper—the original lead singer for Blood, Sweat & Tears. Shattered glass flew everywhere, but what was most disconcerting was the possibility that one of us could've been struck by a ricocheted bullet. (Been calling his band Blood, Sweat and *Bullets* ever since.)

When I ran into Al Kooper some years later, I told him about the David Clayton-Thomas incident. Kooper, to his credit, seemed not the least fazed. "No kidding?" he said, amused. "He had a photo of me *framed*? Was it a *nice* frame?"

I chuckled. "Pewter, I think."

I never asked Kooper what compelled Clayton-Thomas to fire a bullet into his head—photo or otherwise. And I certainly never got around to asking David Clayton-Thomas. When someone, all coked up, whips out a pistol, you don't stick around to ask questions. You get the fuck out of there.

But I digress.

"That was one crazy afternoon," I said to the girl—who, by chance, was named Linda.

"A bummer," she said. Her attention strayed to the inebriated gent finger-drumming on the lip of the bar. "Are you with Keith Moon?" It was apparent she was starstruck.

"He's with me," I said, but with a wink. "That's why I came over to you. He thinks you're Linda Ronstadt. And you gotta admit, the two of you look a lot alike."

"I get that from time to time," she said, using fingernails to comb her long bangs. "I wish I was her."

"And right now's the perfect time," I said. And added, "Just don't sing."

She laughed. "I got laryngitis, I'll tell him," she said, stepping into the role.

I brought her over and introduced them. "Linda, Keith."

"Call me Moonie," he said. He then burped at full volume and, with a comic's precision, fell off the stool.

Rock and roll makes children out of everybody, but Keith was more than just some rock and roll man-child, he was a prankster of the highest order and would do just about anything to elicit a laugh. And laugh she did. She then helped him up, as he knew she would.

"Fall seven times, get up eight," he said, slurring only slightly. "Or izzit the other way around? A *round!*"

The bartender brought over another round. Then another. The more we drank, the more she became the spitting image of Ronstadt. And the more she believed she was.

Keith, not surprisingly, bought it hook, line and Stinger—a cocktail that he made quick work of and ordered another round.

It wasn't long before they became extremely chummy. I had to avert my gaze the moment he worked a hand up her dress, and that's when I spotted on the dance floor two girls, I thought looked familiar, though, in fact, it was just one girl. Keith had gotten me so hammered I was seeing double. I excused myself, but he had his tongue down her throat and took no notice of my leave-taking.

I part-hobbled, part-tottered over to the "two girls" and we danced for what seemed like just a few minutes but, as it turned out, an hour had whizzed by. And by the time I made it back to the bar—the "girls" on my arm—Linda Lookalike and Moonie had left the building.

Never saw him again. In a couple years he would be dead. An accidental overdose. Turned out it wasn't alcohol that killed him, was something prescribed to get him off alcohol.

How fucking ironic.

How fucking sad.

On a slightly lighter note, he more than likely went to his grave thinking he had shagged Linda Ronstadt.

What's more, had he known that he, Keith Moon, the man of all-pranks, got pranked by me, he would've undoubtedly had himself a jolly good laugh.

In triple meter, no less

* * *

EDWIN HEAVEN

1991
BUSTING JAMES BROWN OUT OF PRISON

The phone rang. You might say I answered it "on the one."

"Mr. Heaven!" he crooned in that friendly gravelly voice.

"Mr. Brown!" I replied with unfettered delight.

"Thank you, thank you, thank you," said Mr. Please, Please, Please. "I love what you did!"

He was calling from South Carolina's State Park Correctional Center, where he was serving time for failing to stop for the police in a two-state auto chase. And if you're wondering why James Brown was calling me from the pen, you're not alone. I, too, was wondering.

* * *

When "The World's Biggest Little Film Festival" asked if I would write, direct and produce their trailer, little did I think it would lead to my having a principal role in springing James Brown from prison.

Naturally, when they asked, I was flattered. And why wouldn't I be? In preceding years, the festival's trailer had been written, produced, and directed by the likes of George Lucas and Robin Williams. Albeit, I wasn't the film fest's first choice. That distinction had gone to one John Crawford, a comedy genius along the lines of a Stan Freberg. However, as it turned out (and for reasons I was not privy to), his trailer—a deft parody of *Sunset Boulevard*—got shelved. As a direct consequence, the allotted monies had been spent—it had been quite the production, or so I was told—which left in the coffers very little to speak of, leaving me with no budget and a frightful, drop-dead deadline. So, the idea of hiring a film crew was out of the question. But, as luck would have it, a collection of old-timey previews of coming attractions from the dusty vaults of RKO, Republic, and Monogram Pictures fell on my lap. Sifting through a mile of campy celluloid was an undertaking akin to panning for gold . . . in Cucamonga. But, fortunately, there was gold in them thar reels!

The prevalent theme was the old standby "damsel in distress."

Extreme close-ups of B-movie queens either cornered by a vampire, about to be crushed under the humongous forepaw of a gigantic prehistoric radioactive sea monster or whisked away by a thirty-story tall gorilla—all in glorious black and white and screaming stereophonic. You get the picture. And, like I said, a B-picture.

I cherry-picked the campiest of the camp, pieced them all together and replaced the starlets' bloodcurdling screams with the distinct raspy wail of James Brown. *WHOA-OA-OA!* (The glorious scream that comes right before the verse: "I feel good, I knew that I would, now.")

Having read the inspirational autobiography, *The Godfather of Soul*, I had been considerably moved by the many hardships of young James Joseph Brown and, in some way, wanted to lend a helping hand. And if along the way the trailer got a few laughs, so much the better. As it turned out, it got more than a few.

It began with a booming baritone announcer voice over: "First came Cannes! Then came *bottles*! And now comes the Mill Valley Film Festival . . . *Ten*! The *sequel* to the Mill Valley Film Festival *Nine*! Which is the sequel to Mill Valley Film Festival *Eight*!" And so it went.

The short film ended on a soulful note. While we hear one last James Brown wail—*WHOA-OA-OA!*—a full-screen title card appeared: FREE JAMES BROWN!

It got laughs, applause, and even a few wolf-whistles. (Definitely a hip audience.) Mission accomplished, I drove off into the sunset.

Days later, I transferred film to quarter-inch tape, wrote on the rear side panel of a videocassette the title "Free James Brown" and mailed it to his company Topnotch. (I certainly wasn't about to send it care of the prison. Couldn't risk some overzealous guard tearing it apart in search of contraband.) And so, after dropping it off at the post office, I gave the trailer not another thought.

That is, until that momentous phone call from Soul Brother Number One—now, unfortunately, Inmate Number 155413.

* * *

The call from Mr. Brown had jogged my memory: this wasn't the first time I had sprung a prominent performer from the slammer.

Flashback twenty summers.

I had arrived in California with the intent of producing rock shows at the Monterey Fairgrounds, but ran into more than a few obstacles. Three years prior, the now-famous Monterey Pop, a three-day rock festival, had left the townsfolk shaken. They had been "invaded by hippies"—o! horror of horrors—and it was decreed by the city council there would be no more rock and roll at the fairgrounds, only the customary county fairs and, of course, the jazz festival.

My partner Marguerite Gaffney—the picture of serenity—and I set out to schmooze whomever required some schmoozing. We wined and dined the mayor, police chief, fire chief and even the local chapter of the Hells Angels. It was a Herculean task, but we prevailed. It even made the local news. Being from the Eastern Seaboard, it was an opportunity to book some of our favorite West Coast bands, like Spirit, Love with Arthur Lee, Canned Heat, Chambers Brothers, Lee Michaels and, last but not least, the Steve Miller Band. The latter, unexpectedly, wouldn't take a check, wouldn't even step on stage, until paid the five grand in cash—actually, forty-five hundred, being that we paid an agent his 10% binders fee—which, in 1970, was quite a chunk of change to have on hand (equivalent in today's inflated economy to something like $36,614). And so, like a chicken without its head—or, in my case, without the four thousand-five hundred simoleons—I raced around the fairgrounds trying to come up with the cash. Finally, it dawned on me to ask a couple of the Hell's Angels who were spearheading the security backstage. They said they'd be right back, and ten minutes later they had the moolah. They handed it to Steve Miller, who in turn handed it to his roadie to count. Less than a minute later, Miller walked out onto the stage and that afternoon, as he was apt to do, played a spectacular set and, needless to say, the so-called "hippie" crowd flipped—as did a good number of townsfolk.

That said, the Monterey outdoor concert biz turned out to be a financial bust. But, even so, when I moved to Sausalito shortly after, word got out that I was a bona fide concert producer, which led to my being asked by the Bay Area Venereal Disease Association (BAVDA) to produce a benefit concert. The theme I came up with was "Goodbye VD—A Going Away Party for the Clap." Now, whom could I get to headline such an event? Certainly not the Mormon Tabernacle Choir.

By chance, I came across an album titled *Eric Burdon Declares "War"* and—bingo!—I found my guy. Soon after, we met at the Caravan Lodge in San Francisco's seedy Tenderloin—the motel of choice by gritty rockers and sex workers—and Eric, the former lead singer for the British Invasion band The Animals, and his funk rock backup band War bigheartedly agreed to "declare War on the clap."

Now all we needed was a venue. Enter Bill Graham the Munificent, who provided the Fillmore West for a night.

Next, some top local acts to support the headliner and who better than San Francisco's very own Cockettes, the avant garde drag ensemble comprised of such flamboyant personalities as Divine (who had starred in *Multiple Maniacs,* a John Waters film), Sylvester (the soon-to-be disco star), and such counterculture household names as Scrumbly, Hibiscus and Pristine Condition. The only real drag, however, was Eric Burdon refusing to share the Fillmore's dressing room with transvestites. In spite of having to use a kitchen as a dressing room, the Cockettes weren't the least hampered and, as advertised, they performed the spectacle "Cockettes in Clapland." Arms transformed into eighteen-inch-long papier-mâché penises and concealed in each was a canister of Reddi-wip—so come the grand finale, they whipped-creamed all over the audience.

Also joining the fight against V.D. was Stoneground, a ten-piece band featuring Sal Valentino (Beau Brummels) and the ubiquitous Pete Sears (Hot Tuna, Jefferson Starship). Opening the show was Uncle Vinty, a wonderfully eccentric quick-change artist who accompanied himself on piano and after each snappy number would tear off a layer of clothing until, by the last song, he was down to his radish-red long johns.

"Holy pap smear!" said the emcee Captain Clap (yours truly in the guise of a cartoon superhero I created specifically for the poster). And future Cosmo cover girl Virginia Shaddick, née MacGregor— pure as the driven snow—was crowned "Miss V.D."

And even though it was on a Wednesday evening, a night Bill Graham warned was notoriously slow (and thought I'd be lucky to fill a third of the ballroom), the Fillmore was filled to capacity. And everyone who passed through its doors received a free condom that read: "Spread love, not clap."

So, where am I going with all this? Certainly not the Haight-Ashbury Free Clinic.

Shortly after the "Goodbye V.D." show, Fred Mayer, the friendly Sausalito pharmacist, asked if I'd produce another benefit concert. This time at a brand spanking new venue—the Frank Lloyd Wright inspired Marin Veteran's Memorial Auditorium. It would be the first rock show ever presented there, which, not unlike the situation I had in Monterey, I found most enticing. The theater was deluxe, fully upholstered seats with armrests and entirely air-conditioned, quite a contrast from the standing ballroom at the Fillmore.

Since the concert would be held on Thanksgiving, I billed it as "A 'Cold Turkey' Rock Party"—proceeds going to Marin Open House, a methadone treatment center, and Reach Out, a crisis phone service.

But, once again, I had the somewhat daunting task of finding a headliner to not only perform pro gratis but could also fill two thousand seats. I was told Ron Polte, manager of Quicksilver Messenger Service, was the man to talk to. Quicksilver was a powerful draw, comparable at the time to the Jefferson Airplane, Grateful Dead and Big Brother and the Holding Company. Its band members were a Bay Area "Who's Who"—Nicky Hopkins, Dino Valenti, John Cipollina, Gary Duncan, Greg Elmore, Mark Naftalin and David Freiberg. The latter, an affable fellow with a halo of curls, not only could sing but also played just about every instrument. Problem was, he was sitting in a Redwood City jail cell, busted for possession of pot.

Yes, because of a joint he was in the joint. It was 1971, after all, a time when even a minuscule amount of cannabis could send you up the river.

Polte was the type of band manager who'd go to great lengths to be of service to his musicians, so we banged out a deal, but with one stipulation: if I could use my influence to spring David Freiberg from jail, Quicksilver would headline the concert. If I failed, the deal was off.

So, I composed what I hoped would be a strong case for David's release. I typed it on Lennen & Newell's corporate letterhead. They were one of the country's largest ad agencies and, with Hewlett-Packard as a client, had an ample amount of political clout. Especially in San Mateo County. In the letter, I reasoned that if they released David Freiberg he'd be able to do a hell of a lot more good for the community than rotting in a Redwood City jail cell. He'd be able to perform at a fundraiser for a crisis phone service and methadone treatment center. Without David's participation, however, these two worthy non-profits would likely wind up in deep shit—though not my exact words.

It worked. Freiberg was a free man.

And, not only did Ron Polte keep his word about Quicksilver headlining, he persuaded Big Brother and the Holding Company to be their supporting act. This bill was further strengthened with the addition of Yogi Phlegm (formerly Sons of Champlin, another Bay

Area darling managed by Polte) and Clover (Huey Lewis' first band). Brilliant cartoonist Jerry McDonald created a wacky poster featuring groupies, narcs and sunbathing aardvarks, and we plastered this baby all over Marin. The rest, as they say, is rock and roll hysteria.

One particular moment I have not forgotten was after Yogi Phlegm's set when a little wisp of a gal in a tight tank top and faded denims wandered on stage. She looked no more than sixteen and thinking she was some groupie who had slipped past security, I started to escort her off the stage.

"Whoa, dude!" she laughed. "I sing lead for Big Brother!"

Though never will there be another Janis Joplin, Kathi McDonald that night came awfully darn close.

It was the night, some say, the Marin Veteran's Memorial Auditorium lost its rock and roll cherry and, surprisingly, only a half dozen of the two thousand plush seats were destroyed. Apart from the ghost of Frank Lloyd Wright who was probably pulling his translucent hair, everyone in attendance seemed to have a rockin' good Thanksgiving.

But none smiled more that night than Mr. Freiberg.

Which brings us back to Mr. Brown.

*　*　*

I imagined he, too, was smiling that morning we chatted for what must've been a good half-hour, mostly about music, film and our kids. Of the latter, he had something like ten that he knew of and a procession of past lovers with DNA petitions.

I mentioned I had a little girl. "She's seven," I said. "Audrey."

"Audrey Heaven? With a name like that, she'll go far."

"She may be little but she's a big James Brown fan. Further proof you're an American institution!"

"I like that better than a penal institution."

"I showed her The *T.A.M.I. Show*."

"My favorite! That's the greatest in the world! But it's tiring just to look at it."

I laughed. "And that's coming from the man that did six shows a day at the Apollo!"

"You gotta be superhuman," he yelped, "you gotta be superhuman!"

I tried to picture what this superhuman looked like on the other end of the line. They probably made him wear one of those bright orange jumpsuits. That familiar conk pompadour of his was most likely unconked and bereft of pomp. (Unless he pulled a few strings and arranged for one of those professional hooded hair dryers be placed in his cell.) And even without clunky heels, I imagined he still stood tall—the tallest five-foot-four man in his cellblock. I also pictured his trusted valet Danny Ray showing up on visitor's day to drape a full-sized satin cape around Mr. Brown's shoulders, like he always did during the performance of "Please, Please, Please."

Incidentally, I had no idea he would be calling till the night before, when his wife Adrienne Rodriguez phoned to say Mr. Brown would be calling at eight a.m. to thank me. Which took me by surprise.

"Calling me?"

"You *are* Edwin Heaven?"

"Uh-huh."

"Then yes, he's calling you."

She went on to tell me he prefers being addressed as Mr. Brown. This I knew, having read his autobiography. The way it was explained in the book, black people were commonly addressed by their first names while white folks were shown respect by referring to one another by their surname. "Mister So-And-So, meet Mr. So-And-So." But when a white man was introduced to a black man, it was "Mr. So-And-So, meet James." So, it was requested he be called Mr. Brown. Out of respect. An emotion Aretha Franklin felt so strongly about, she spelled it out. R-E-S-P-E-C-T!

And so, after helping prepare scrambled eggs and beans for about a hundred and fifty fellow inmates, The Hardest Working Man in Show Biz (and Prison Kitchens) called me. About twenty minutes into the call, I told him about a young lady here in San Francisco name of Dee Russell who did a show she called "The Church of James Brown."

"WHAAT?!" It was as if he'd just received a gubernatorial pardon.

"If she knew I was talking to you about her," I said, "she'd probably die and go to heaven."

"Well, you see this young lady, you tell her I love her."

"She saw you perform at the Fairmont Hotel in the Venetian Room," I said, "and was totally blown away."

"When you see me at the Fairmont, that's one of my enjoyable performances," he said. "It's where I can reach back and sing songs I normally don't get a chance to sing, where I could utilize their big band to do some other numbers, you know?"

"Like what?"

"I did things like 'Night and Day.' I did 'Strangers in The Night.' I did 'Only You.' I did 'These Foolish Things.' I did 'My Way,' all those Sinatra things. And 'Prisoner of Love.'"

"Speaking of which," I said, and told him of another idea I had been toying with to help get him sprung. An album featuring an array of famous recording artists interpreting "Prisoner of Love" in their own distinct style—along with, of course, James Brown's famous rendition. Some of the artists mentioned were Linda Ronstadt, Prince, and MC Hammer. I told him I thought it might boost public opinion, maybe further influence the penal authorities, and asked what he thought.

"It's a damn good idea," he said. "It's creative and it's artistic. It's what the future could be about. All of us pulling together for a better, brighter world . . . I *like* it." And then, as if to further express his appreciation, he said, "Look, when I get out, I'd like to show your film to a lot of people around the country. Maybe on some television shows. Things like that. It just makes me feel good."

"And when *you* 'feel good,' Mr. Brown, we all 'get up offa that thing!'"

He chuckled. "You seem to be one of those people who got that spark. We gotta keep that light burnin'." The way he said it, it could've been a lyric in one of his songs. "I want to share something with you," he continued. "I'm on my way now for either a pardon or unsupervised parole, and when I get out I'm goin' on *The Arsenio Hall Show.* He told me when I come back, I'll always have a home on his show, and, when I do, I'm gonna thank you, personally, in front of all of America."

Dumbstruck, I became lost in thought: *What a sweet guy. There ought to be a Crayola crayon called "Mr. Brown," and that football team in Cleveland ought to be called the "Mr. Browns," and brownies ought to be called . . .*

"Well, looky here," he said, rousing me from my reverie. "I'm gonna let you go. Thanks again for the 'Free James Brown.' Kiss the baby for me, and may God bless you for what you did and with what you're doing."

"Thank you for calling. It was very kind of you," I said. "Bye-bye." (Eep! I said "bye-bye" as if I'd been talking to my kid, or mom, or a hoarse Mr. Rogers.)

"So long," said Mr. Brown.

When later that year he was released, three years shy of the full six-year term, I wasn't unrealistic. I knew that my goofy little "Free James Brown" film was only one of many efforts to persuade the penal authorities to grant an early release. Many others had pitched in. The "Free James Brown" movement, for example, had been originated by a record producer and a rap artist—Van Silk and Mellie Mel, respectively—and hundreds of others pulled together hoping to get a million signatures. And so forth. Nonetheless, it was still very kind of him to call and treat me as if I was the only one. And though I'm certain he called others that morning, none could possibly have been more pleased, pleased, pleased than me.

And so, the big night arrived.

Audrey had my permission to stay up past her bedtime to watch The Arsenio Hall Show. She had a vested interest, after all, having performed automated dialogue replacement on the trailer. (One of her scenes takes place in a war room. An astronomer warns of a comet the size of Staten Island on a collision course with Earth. A barrel-chested general speaks out, but instead of the audience hearing the actor's gruff manly voice, it's the petite little voice of a five-year-old girl. "I never did like Staten Island," she says. It got one of the biggest laughs.)

Now seven years old, she's watching the telly beside her dad as "Mr. Dynamite" struts and slides across Paramount Studio's Stage 29, then does a series of spins and splits as he wails . . .

> *Get up (get on up)*
> *Get up (get on up)*

The studio audience went wild—as did Audrey and me.

James Brown then took a seat next to Arsenio. "Welcome

home," said the popular late-night host. "It's great to have you back."

"Thank heaven!" said James Brown.

Audrey looked at me. "Dad! He just thanked you!"

"I think he was just thanking God or the heavens above."

"Then he would've *said* 'God' or 'the heavens above.' He just said 'thank Heaven!' Just like he said he would."

"Don't you think he would've then said 'thank *Edwin* Heaven' or '*Mr.* Heaven? Not just 'heaven?'"

"Why not? Your friends call you Heaven." She had a point there. "Or maybe he couldn't remember your first name."

"At least he didn't call me Edward."

"Or Googy," she giggled. "Maybe all the people watching are supposed to think he's thanking the heavens above, but *he* knows that *you* know he's thanking *you*, Dad. He's just being really cool about it."

This coming from a seven-year-old! Yeah, I'm thinking, James Brown may be one cool hombre, but so is my kid.

"Who cares if everyone else watching thinks he's thanking the heavens," I said, "you and I know he's thanking The Heavens." Then, as an afterthought, "The man's word is pure gold."

"I like silver better," she said, straight-faced.

I laughed and threw an arm around her. "Me, too, you little comedian. Now off to bed. School tomorrow. Gotta get up!"

"Get on up!" she said, imitating him in a cute gravelly voice. And on the way to bed she did a funny little James Brown move. "Get on up!"

It was apparent she'd been bitten by the acting bug. Probably while helping me on the trailer. And, in a few more years, she'll be discovered by Sofia Coppola, and star in Sofia's directorial debut.

But—*good God, y'all!* That's another story.

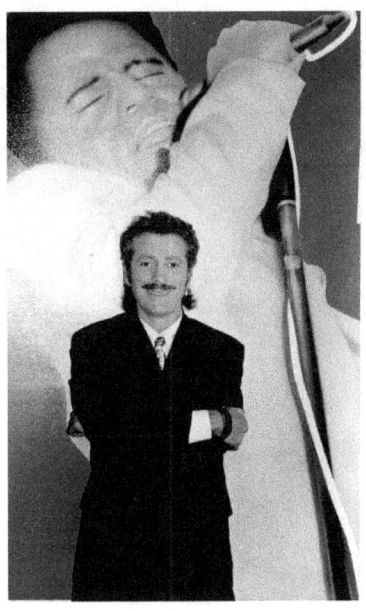

Mr. Heaven and Mr. Brown

* * *

1983

THE SINCEREST FORM OF FLATULENCE

Back when I was writing for Rich Little, the great impressionist, he farted.

I said, "Wow, Rich, that sounded just like Humphrey Bogart!"

We laughed and struck matches.

Rich could impersonate anyone. I had a ball writing for him. Whether it was Bogey, Jack Benny, Cary Grant, Gary Cooper, Clark Gable, James Cagney, Fred McMurray, Bing Crosby, Bob Hope, Frank Sinatra, Dean Martin, Sammy Davis, Jr., Johnny Carson, ad nauseam. You name it, Rich did it. (He once tried to imitate my Uncle Irving, but it sounded more like my Aunt Matilda.)

Whenever I sat down to write for Rich, I felt like the head of a motion picture studio. At my fingertips was an all-star cast, a hit parade of characters, the entire Hollywood Walk of Fame.

Here's a fun little fact: Rich Little could do a Little Richard impression, but Little Richard couldn't do a Rich Little impression. And the Impressions couldn't do either.

One of Rich's best impressions was his rendition of George Burns.

At one recording session, I was outside the studio catching a breather (which in smoggy L.A. is a joke in itself), when a limo pulled up in front and out stepped George Burns. Since he would eventually live to be a hundred, at the time of this encounter he had to be about eighty-eight. He was hunched over and looked even littler than he did on the big screen. Between thumb and forefinger was his trademark cigar. The man reeked of class (and cigar smoke).

"Oh, God!" I said, knowing he probably hears this wisecrack time after time, but he grins, nonetheless.

"Hello, kid."

"Mr. Burns . . ."

He cut me off. "Call me George. My father was Mr. Burns." He paused. Fiddled with his cigar. "That's not true. Actually, he was Mr. Birnbaum."

Kibbitzing, I told him I was toying with an idea for a script about a 400-foot George Burns brought back to life by a nuclear accident. "Calling it 'Oh, Godzilla!'"

He gave me his classic "straight man" grin, so I proceeded to tell him I'm producing Rich Little in Studio A and that he ought to stop by. "Rich really nails you."

"Sounds painful," he said. He chuckled, then said, "Sonny, I'd like to, but I'm on my way to do some ADR, which we didn't have in the days of silent films, and am running late." Took a puff of his cigar and added, "And I haven't run in forty years."

An idea hit me.

Once, at another Rich Little session, I ran into a friend, Terry McGovern, the popular San Francisco morning jock on KSAN-FM. He was now getting acting roles and voiceover work in Hollywood, and I recalled him doing a pretty decent impression of George Burns. So, strictly on a whim, he and I decided to pull a little prank on Mr. Little, because I knew Rich was someone who not only could deliver a joke, but could also take one. I had Terry call the studio we were recording in and told Rich it was George Burns calling. Terry did about ten seconds or so of George on the phone, but Rich didn't fall for it—to be a great impressionist, you had to have a great ear—but, nonetheless, we all got a good laugh out of it.

So now, here I was with the real George Burns, a man known to like a little mischief now and then.

I told him if he wasn't too busy, to stop by, I got a funny idea.

"I'm all ears," he grinned, took a puff of his cigar, and with perfect comic timing added, "as you can plainly see."

We entered the lobby in step. They were little steps. Before heading off in different directions, he gave me a conspiratorial wink. He shuffled past the receptionist and said something that made her laugh. Hers was an affable laugh, one I remembered from another session.

I had written for and produced Jonathan Winters, a sheer joy to work with, but more than a bit loony. On that particular day, he was wearing his USMC jacket, rank of corporal (although he was wearing a general's cap), and since this certain receptionist was exceptionally easy on the eyes, Jonathan began improvising. Had her laughing her ass off, and I was pretty sure Jonathan was hoping, given enough time, she'd maybe laugh her entire ensemble off. But since, at the time, he was powered by lithium, I had to coax him away before he'd wear himself out. Experience had taught me that I had about a half hour window of comic mania before fatigue would set in. Before parting, he gave her a sharp salute.

"Semper fi!" he said.

And she gave him the "Guns Up" sign.

Which is what I did before entering Studio A.

"Aww, you remembered," I heard her say.

How could I possibly forget?

Ten minutes later, I was seated at the console next to my engineer, Rich was behind the soundproof window standing at the mic, when the phone rang. I picked it up, said hello, hit the push-to-talk button on the intercom and said, "Hey, Rich? Some guy says he does a better George Burns than Rich Little. Better pick up line three."

Edwin Heaven and Rich Little · Photo: Joe Tarsia

Rich snickered. He was thinking, probably, *Oh boy, Edwin's at it again!* He picked up, and in his best George Burns said, "Still shooting pool with a rope, kid?" He listened for a beat or two, rolled his eyes and in his normal voice said, although not unkindly, "Not a bad impression, pal. I've heard much worse. Needs a little work though. You know what they say, practice makes perfect." Then switching back to his perfect George Burns impression said, "Now, say goodnight, Gracie."

Soon as he hung up, he looked over at me and said in his spot-on Jack Benny voice, "Well! That's got to be one of the *saddest* George Burns impressions I've *ever* heard."

I couldn't believe my ears and thought it best to keep the identity of the caller to myself. At least, till the end of our session. But now that I've had some time to think about it, maybe Rich knew all along. And, maybe, it was I who got pranked.

EDWIN HEAVEN

2002

FRANCIS, GEORGE, AND
A DUCK NAMED HOWARD

Once while having cocktails with Francis Coppola and George Lucas at Rouge, a San Francisco nightclub, Francis said to George, "You know, maybe you should've stuck to Edwin's script." Francis said this with an impish twinkle and, obviously, was yanking his good buddy's chain.

I was sipping a Martini at the time and nearly choked to death on the cocktail pick - olive and all. George didn't seem fazed, as if he and Francis had forever yanked one another's chain.

"I'm afraid *Howard the Duck* was before my time," George said, passing the buck, as they say. (Actually, passing $37 million bucks, almost as much as the entire *Star Wars* trilogy cost to make.)

"I'll drink to that!" I said, gingerly removing the toothpick from my uvula.

"I'll quack to that," said Francis. "Quack."

"Howard didn't quack," I said. "He talked."

"All characters talk, but few have anything to say," said Francis, while toying with my A.T. Cross Ion pen. It was shaped like a plump silver rocket from an old Buck Rogers movie. (Later, he would hand me his pen, and pocket mine. I was okay with that, since engraved on that shiny little pen in uppercase block letters were those legendary words: EDWIN HEAVEN WRITES LIKE HELL.)

"I doubt if even Paddy Chayefsky," continued Francis, "could've saved that movie."

Now, the odd thing was—though, I didn't bring it up at the time—back in 1981, when Stan Lee and I had our story sessions at Marvel and would get tangled by a particularly dark or tricky scene, I'd say, "Wonder what Chayefsky would do?"

And Stan would offer me a bowl of M&M's, and say, "Probably help himself to a handful."

George could only stay for a drink, then said his goodbyes, had to be somewhere—perhaps the planet Dagobah—and slid out of the booth. As he walked past, I handed him my card.

"My card," I said, "in case you found me charming."

Francis laughed and George slipped the card into a pocket. So, that's how it's done here in "Hollywood North."

But, getting back to the M&M's thing. Let me explain.

Back in '81, indie producers Peter Shanaberg, Morrie Eisenman and Peter Cofrin had acquired screen rights for Howard the Duck and, having read some of my funnier scripts, hired me to write a first draft and flew me out to Hollywood for a story meeting with Marvel's Stan Lee.

Being newlyweds, I brought along my wife. Stan, the consummate host, brought out a bowl of trail mix and a bowl of M&M's. He asked us to choose. She opted for the trail mix, and I the M&M's. Stan then offered a choice of two beverages. Coca Cola or apple juice. She went for the apple juice, and I the Coke.

"Good thing your husband's writing this script," he kibitzed, and we laughed.

But, had it been some kind of test? Was the Howard the Duck fan base not what you'd call your trail mix and apple juice type? Oh well, it mattered not, because little did we know at the time, that all the M&M's and coke in the world wouldn't save Howard. It became a $37 million-dollar flop and a Woody Allen punchline: "The three greatest movies," said Woody, "are *Citizen Kane, Casablanca* and *Howard the Duck.*"

Alan Parker, a pretty darn good director (look him up), once said it's just as hard to make a bad movie as a good one, and no one sets out to make a bad movie. Yet, when *Howard the Duck* was finally released, no one could've imagined that the man who created *Star Wars* and *Indiana Jones* could possibly have helmed such a clunker.

George Lucas, a comic book aficionado, certainly didn't set out to turn his favorite duck into a turkey. But shit happens. The Force ain't always with you. He had originally visualized Howard the Duck as an animated film, but Universal Pictures—in this case, the dark side of the Force—insisted the film be live-action. Wouldn't green-light it, unless it was.

And so, it came to pass, in order to make Howard's cigar-chomping face chomp, Industrial Light & Magic was compelled to use animatronic puppetry. If it had been *Howard the Muppet*, it might've worked. But, puppetry stifled Howard's a cting chops. Made him a lame duck.

It had been the intention of Stan Lee, the driving force behind Marvel Comics, to have this webbed-footed "Master of Quack Fu" designed by special-effects w izard S tan Winston, t he d ude who created Yoda. The clay models Winston showed us that afternoon, back in '81, were closer in temperament with the humanoid duck created by writer Steve Gerber and artist Val Myerick. It had film noir characteristics. Howard, a cynical absurdist, was a feathery little badass not to be fucked with. Yet, as it turned out, the duck got fucked and plucked.

At the premiere, midway into the film (or, to be precise, halfway through a movie-theater-sized box of M&M's), I had had enough and walked out.

And, alongside me, walked Howard.

Howard the Duck clay model by Stan Winston

* * *

1968

ONCE UPON A PIGLET

I was slicing an Italian roll with a knife ten times sharper than a razor blade, when—whoops!—it sliced straight through the roll like melted butter and into the fleshiest part of my hand. If you're into palmistry, you might say my lifeline looked like a scaled-down parting of the Red Sea.

My idea of a New Year's celebration wasn't sitting in the ER waiting for stitches, so, instead, I wrapped a linen napkin tightly around the gory gash and, to reduce the flow of blood, made a fist and held it high above my head.

At that very moment, the neighborhood went bonkers, signaling midnight.

"Happy fucking New Year!" I grumbled and stepped outside for a smoke.

It seemed as if every Tom, Dick, and Guido was firing handguns into the midnight sky. It was a South Philly tradition, supposedly dating back to the days of muzzle-loading muskets. One of the trigger-happy revelers gave me the old stink eye, apparently mistaking my raised fist pose for the black power salute. Therefore, being that this part of town was notoriously racist and he was brandishing a smoking revolver, I thought it wise to haul ass. After all, wouldn't want to be mistaken for the midnight sky.

It certainly was not what you'd call an auspicious start to a new year. But, as the expression goes, out of bad comes good. And, good golly, there she was, just walking down the street, singing *"do wah diddy, diddy, dum diddy do"*—or something to that effect—and my heart raced like Man O' War at Churchill Downs.

She was the prettiest damn thing I ever did see. Sort of resembled the famous Brit model Jean Shrimpton. Or, with her porcelain skin—excuse the histrionics—maybe a mythological beauty from Ancient Greece. (I believe back then they wore miniskirts, too.)

Helen of Troy, meet Millie of Philly.

Her looks had me reeling with the feeling (as Bobby Darin once sang), but, it was her jolly laugh that plunked my heartstrings. How could someone so slender have a fat lady laugh? It was as if at the center of her being was a Jolly Dolly Dimples. Or, maybe, a Mrs. Claus.

No denying, I was smitten. Madly in smit. Couldn't say "love," because, as luck would have it, she had a boyfriend—one much older, cooler, and hairier than me.

But, that wouldn't stop us from becoming fast friends.

Then came the day we were hanging out, talking about favorite authors, and the topic shifted from the love letters of F. Scott Fitzgerald to the children's books of A.A. Milne and her long-standing fondness for Piglet, the baby pig and best friend of Winnie-the-Pooh.

And *shtoink!*—an idea sprang forth.

I would do something no boyfriend, past or present, was cuckoo enough to do. At the time, I saw it as a romantic gesture. Something akin to a Scott Fitzgerald love letter.

And so—that weekend I drove to a pig farm way the fuck out in the sticks of New Jersey and told the pig farmer I wanted to surprise a girl with a piglet.

"Either you're crazy about this girl," he said, "or just plain crazy."

"Both," I said.

He had on a well-worn Phillies cap that I took as a good omen. Millie's dad was a Phillies coach. The pig farmer led me past a string of sties that smelled not the least like the perfume counter at Wanamaker's Department Store. At last, we came to one of the nursery pens. The piglets—huddled—were all the same size and age. Eight weeks. It was then and there I decided never would I eat one. Just the thought of a BLT saddened me. They were all so damn cute. It wasn't easy picking one, so I chose the pinkest among the bunch. I handed the pig farmer his fifteen bucks and he put the lucky piglet in a burlap bag, mud and all.

I gently placed it in the back of my MGB GT hatchback.

"Millie's gonna love you," I said in a soothing voice, the one I used for tiny puppies. "And vice versa."

When I got to the tollbooth at the approach to the Ben Franklin Bridge, the burlap bag started moving all around in the back of the car.

"What's in the bag, sir?" inquired the toll collector as if, for all she knew, I had abducted a small child.

"A pig." I said it as if a scuttling pig in a burlap bag must be commonplace for toll collectors.

"Oh, okay," she said, mater-of-factly. Then added, "Bon appétit!"

"I'm a vegetarian," I said, and drove off.

Soon as I got to my downtown apartment, I bathed it, powdered it like it was a baby's tush, and tied a big red bow around its neck.

"Oink," it said.

"Good, I'm glad you like."

Millie was, naturally, surprised.

Unfortunately, so was her landlord.

I later found out she got evicted. I found out, also, that as she was riding the Frankford El to her mother's house, piglet cradled in her arms, she was cited. Evidently, and unbeknownst to me, there was a city ordinance banning farm animals as pets.

I hadn't thought it through, obviously. Had I, no way would I have saddled Millie with such a burden (adorable as it was) to feed and care for a piglet at a time when she could hardly care for herself.

The little pig lived at her mom's house, till it was no longer little. Millie was then forced to take the large pig—now known as McGregor—to a farm, but not without an arrangement in place: he would not be killed.

Indeed, it was a loony tunes idea giving her a piglet. Although, I admit, some good came from it: the little piglet I had chosen to come home with me, unlike the others, had steered clear of the slaughterhouse.

I lost touch with Millie the following year when I moved to California.

Decades later, though, we reconnected, and I finally confessed that, once upon a piglet, I had been madly in love with her.

"Why didn't you *tell* me?"

"I gave you a pig, for god sakes!" I said. "If *that* isn't a tell, what is?"

* * *

EDWIN HEAVEN

2002
THE SEXY BEAST AND SOME GUY NAMED PHIL

One night following a private screening of the gangster film *Sexy Beast,* we all met up in the backroom of Tosca Café. By "we" I'm talking Francis and Eleanor Coppola, Sean Penn and Robin Wright, and the recently knighted star of the aforementioned mobster film Ben Kingsley. Sir Ben's performance of a loose cannon Cockney mob enforcer had been such a convincing portrayal that my date, a striking model and sometime film extra (or, as she preferred, "background talent"), was apprehensive about meeting him, and I had to remind her that this was the same bloke who played Gandhi.

Tosca's backroom was where San Francisco's café society— mainly the film and literary crowd—could congregate in private. Shoot pool, shoot the shit, or shoot whatever it was their pleasure.

Standing not far from its private entrance stood Robin Wright, the beautiful screen star. She had on a pink and "robin's egg blue" plaid shirt—cool in a Curt Cobain way. Tosca's long wooden bar wasn't far from where she stood, which is why my date mistook her for a barmaid.

"A Cosmopolitan, please," she said to Robin.

"Ahem," I ahem'd, more or less mortified, "this is Robin Wright, Mary. She's not a waitress, she's a princess."

Robin, with a big, kindly smile, said she didn't mind getting her a drink, and would I like a Cosmo, too.

I didn't want to put her out, but she gave me a look as if to say, *Don't be a schmuck, Edwin, it's just as easy for me to bring over two drinks as it is one.* So I said okay, thanked her and started to reach into my pocket for some dough, but she waved it off, said the Kingsley party is being comped by Jeannette (the grand dame who runs the joint).

The backroom was just large enough to accommodate a pool table and two rows of straight back chairs facing each another. There were two doors. The one we entered from the bar, and the other which led to the restroom. There was enough aisle space between the two rows of chairs to make a mad dash to the latter without stepping on any toes. Francis, Ellie and Sir Ben, with backs to the wall, sat across from Sean, Robin, my date and me. On the walls were movie posters, its directors Tosca regulars. Philip Kaufman (*The Right Stuff*), Win Wenders (*Paris, Texas*), George Lucas (*Star Wars*) and Francis Ford Coppola (*Apocalypse Now*).

The conversation had gotten around to Sir Ben's "boogie man" character in Sexy Beast and how he cussed like a motherfucker. *You fuckin honkin jam-rag fuckin spunk-bubble!* And so on. Francis asked who we all thought had the foulest mouth in Hollywood. There were a few good guesses that were close—Tallulah Bankhead and Oliver Reed—but no cigar.

And then I whooped like a schoolboy who suddenly knew the capital of Paraguay, "Fred Astaire!" Which came as a surprise to everyone but Francis.

I had read somewhere, probably in some vintage issue of *Confidential* (the magazine that " Tells t he F acts A nd Names T he Names") that Astaire had quite the potty mouth. It also didn't' hurt that I knew Francis had directed Astaire in *Finian's Rainbow*.

On the studio's back lot, according to Francis, the debonair leading man of such Hollywood classics as *Top Hat* and *Funny Face* could cuss a streak of blue that would make George Carlin sound like Father Fitzgibbon. Francis asked if I knew how Astaire had become so adept at cussing.

I took a stab at it. "Because he started out in vaudeville?"

Vaudeville was not the most wholesome environment for a seven-year-old hoofer.

Then Mary, my date, suddenly blurted something that had not a thing to do with Astaire or vaudeville or, for that matter, "fuckin spunk-bubbles." No one objected though, since she hadn't made a peep until now and was probably feeling a bit left out of the conversation.

"I once had a walk-on in a Robert De Niro film," she said, "and when I called him Mr. De Niro, he said, 'Just call me Bobby Dee.'"

After a brief silence, Francis said, "And you can call me Fat Frankie."

Sean, returning from the powder room and feeling frisky, wanted to know what was so funny.

"Ask 'Fat Frankie,'" Mary said, and again the backroom filled with laughter.

Then Sean soon had us all in stitches. He was, without question, one of our finest dramatic actors, but aside from his Jeff Spicoli character in *Fast Times at Ridgemont High*, I had no idea he was so funny. I'm talking *Robin Williams funny*. If the aisle hadn't been so narrow, we would've all been rolling in it. What I mostly recall is a joke he told. It's a hell of a lot funnier coming out of his mouth, but it went something like this:

"Some guy is marooned on a desert island with Elle Macpherson, the famous swimsuit model. He plays it cool at first, not making any moves on Elle for several weeks. Finally, he asks if they could start a physical relationship, to attend to each other's needs. Elle is likeminded and a very nice sexual relationship begins. After several months, he says to her, 'Elle, I have a problem. It's kind of a guy thing, but I need to ask a favor of you.' She replies, 'Okay.' To which he asks, 'Can I borrow your eyebrow pencil?' She looks at him in confusion, but obliges. The guy then asks, 'Do you mind if I use it to draw a mustache on you?' Elle, though still confused and, by now, mildly concerned, once again obliges. So, he draws a mustache on her. One of those parted pencil-thin kind that exposes her exquisite philtrum. You know that come-hither dimple on the center of her upper lip. Then he says, 'Can you wear some of my clothes? I need for you to look more like a man.' Elle is hesitant, but nonetheless puts on his clothes. Finally, the guy says to Elle, 'Do you mind if I call you Phil?' Though not exactly thrilled, she relents. 'If that's what you want,' she says, 'then go ahead, you can call me Phil.' So, the guy reaches out and grabs her by the arms and shouts, 'PHIL! YOU'LL NEVER BELIEVE WHO I'M FUCKING!'"

Later, my date would express displeasure with the joke. She couldn't believe that Sean had told that joke using Elle Macpherson's name in front of his wife. *Elle was a former girlfriend,* she explained. I tried to explain that the joke wouldn't have worked had he substituted Robin's name for Elle's, because if he was marooned on an island with his wife why would he need to draw a mustache on her and call her "Phil" just so he could tell this imaginary Phil he was fucking his *wife?* Mary still didn't think Sean's joke was all that funny. That is, not till much later that night when I went down on her and asked, "May I call you Phil?"

But, again, I digress.

As we were leaving the backroom, after we had all said our goodbyes, I mentioned to Robin, in way of a compliment, that she still looked every bit as lovely as she did when she played Buttercup in *Princess Bride.* She thanked me with a big smile. I mean, who doesn't like a little flattery? And it wasn't at all as if I was coming on to her.

Nonetheless—Sean gave me the ol' hairy eyeball.

Either that, or had a cinder in his eye.

But, I didn't stick around to find out.

* * *

THE NIGHT I GOT DAVID BOWIE LAID *sorta*

EDWIN HEAVEN

1997

A LITTLE ROBIN STORY

My initial introduction to Robin Williams, the brilliant comic and Oscar-winning actor, was back in '76 at the Tubes' Talent Hunt.

Still an unknown, Robin auditioned along with a hundred other contestants. Winners would get to perform onstage alongside the Tubes, who at the time were the hottest and most outrageous live show in the city, if not the world. And, as astonishing as this might sound, Robin Williams had gotten the hook.

He wore a cowboy hat, fluffy chaps and a brassier, while strumming a guitar and singing a zany song about growing breasts. "I've got the hormonal blues," Robin sang.

"Sorry, Contestant Number 27," said celebrity judge Martin

Mull (this was years before he would costar with Robin in *Mrs. Doubtfire*), "but the Tubes have more than enough guitar players!"

Well, hell—we all know the rest of the story. Two years after the Tubes' Talent Hunt, Robin got his own TV show, *Mork and Mindy*, and became an "overnight" sensation—a rocket to the moon (or, should we say, the planet Ork).

Robin knew me not just through the Tubes, but also Herb Caen, the king of "three dot" journalism. And over the years, Robin and I would occasionally run into one another, like at a wedding or a memorial.

The wedding was Monica Gannas' (of Rick & Ruby fame). At the wedding reception, held at the old California Club on Clay Street, Robin blew my mind when he recalled (almost verbatim) a one-liner of mine that wound up as a blurb in Herb's column. It read: "'Marin County,' snorts Edwin Heaven disgustedly, 'is where they stuff all kinds of stuff up their noses but give you dirty looks for putting sugar in your coffee . . . '" Robin made it sound even funnier by verbalizing the ellipsis: "Dot dot dot."

And the memorial was for Herb Caen.

"Being a famous journalist," said Robin, when it was his turn at the pulpit, "is kind of like being the best-dressed woman on radio."

It brought down the house—or should I say, the cathedral.

Though it was a day to grieve, he had lifted our spirits—a knack he had in spades. Hearts, clubs and diamonds, as well. When Steven Spielberg was filming *Schindler's List* in Krakow—once a ghetto created by the Nazis where many tens of thousands of men, women and children were carted away in holocaust trains to Auschwitz, where they would be exterminated—he called Robin during the darkest of nights when he needed a ray of light. Robin, in his inimitable way, managed to make the great director laugh by telling him he was "representing People for the Valdheimer's Association, a society devoted to helping raise money for older Germans who had forgotten everything before 1945."

Robin and I left Herb's memorial together. Robin was besieged on the steps of Grace Cathedral by a small army of paparazzi and TV news correspondents, a dozen cameras and microphones barely a foot away from his face, and from behind one of the cameras came this snide remark: "Robin! How's the herpes?"

It was nothing but a mean dig. Some ass-rag member of the press was trying to provoke Robin, hoping to get a rise out of him, a story for the tabloids, perhaps. But to Robin's credit, he never lost his cool or dropped his smile. Robin replied ever so politely, as we broke through the crunch of cameras. "They're fine, thank you."

As we're headed up California Street to the Fairmont Hotel for the post-memorial reception—lift a few "Vitamin V" martinis in Herb's honor (vodka being Herb's vitamin of choice)—I said to Robin, "Wow, how'd you do that? Remain so calm and detached? That guy was asking for a poke in the nose."

"Naah," said Robin. "That would've only given the asshole a story. And the story, here, today, is Herb."

And I added, for good measure: "Dot dot *dot!*"

THE NIGHT I GOT DAVID BOWIE LAID *sorta*

EDWIN HEAVEN

1994

MOBSTERS, THEY'RE ALWAYS IN SEASON

The House of Nanking, a Shanghai-styled hole in the wall, was always packed with a constant line outside, dishes clattering, and people chattering in assorted languages. The three of us sat at the counter. I had brought along a gal from Nebraska who had moved in with me, and apparently had decided it would be for an indefinite stay. I wasn't complaining, not in the least. She was a real beauty and sweet as honey. Hers was one of those long, graceful necks you'd see on Bolshoi ballerinas or those Ndebele tribal women. Her breasts were spectacular, and I could almost fit my hands around her waist (hands that couldn't palm a basketball, mind you). *How was such a slender waist possible, when her appetite was that of a lumberjack's?*

She was seated to my left, perusing a large, laminated menu.

On my right sat Francis Ford Coppola. She had no idea who he was, at least not by sight, and I hadn't told her. I just said we're going to grab a bite with a friend.

"I could really go for a bite," she said.

I'm sure you could, I was thinking, you gorgeous lumberjack.

She knew little about films (called them "picture shows"), so, to make conversation, she asked the man with the salt-and-pepper beard what he did for a living.

Francis, who could kid with the best, said he owned a furniture store.

"Frankie's Furniture," he said, deadpan. "I'm Frankie."

Not to ruin his game, but didn't want to keep my girlfriend completely in the dark, I said, "Does that mean, 'Frankie', your next 'picture show' is *The Bedroom Set?*"

Maybe she didn't know much about screenwriters and directors or producing 'picture shows,' but knew scrumptious food when she smelled it, and ordered as if for a football team.

Francis grinned and said he'd pay for the meals if I paid for the drinks.

"Deal," I said, thinking I was getting the better part of the arrangement. Surely, the three of us would be eating more than we drank, especially the way I've seen Miss Nebraska put it away.

I would soon discover, however, that when it came to guzzling Tsingtao, she had few rivals.

As the three of us consumed enormous portions of Nanking Sesame Chicken, Spicy Szechuan Chicken with Hot Peppers, Zesty Potstickers with peanut sauce, and whatnot, while downing one icy cold Tsingtao after another, after another, I told him about *The Lobster and The Mobster*, a story I had written in the Runyonesque vernacular style, and asked if he thought it would make for a good movie.

"Well, mobsters . . ." Francis said, between bites of fiery-hot shrimp cakes and gulps of Chinese beer, "they are always in season. But try to find a good lobster when you need one!"

The check arrived. He glanced at it and chuckled. Being a Nanking regular (his building sits right across the street from the restaurant), he knew (after many a lunch) that the spicy-hot fare required countless bottles of beer to put out the fire.

I reached into my pocket to pay the lion's share, but Francis waved me off, said he'd get it—all of it.

"You're a saint, Francis."

"Saint Francis?" he laughed. "I wouldn't go *that* far."

Then he told me that his mother, *mammarella* he called her, had told him when he was a little boy, "Your brother Augie is the smart one, your sister Talia is the pretty one and, you, Francis, you're the *kind* one."

"*Mammarella* is right," I said. "You are without doubt the kind one." Then added, "Except perhaps when it comes to lobsters."

"Touché," grinned Francis.

"Tsingtao!" burped Miss Nebraska.

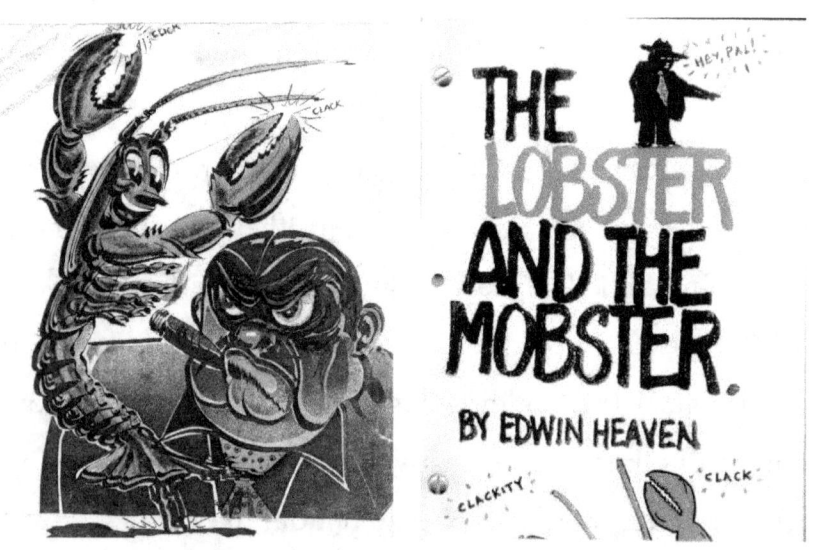

Art by Prairie Prince and Edwin Heaven

* * *

EDWIN HEAVEN

1976
McCOOL

Steve McQueen was a nice guy, a cool guy, a guy's guy—and, from what I could tell, a friendly dude. (Back then, we called everybody dude.)

I met him and Ali MacGraw one sunny afternoon in Sausalito. At the time, I had two Afghan Hounds—Ben and Sally—and a huge Afro. (I looked like I played bass in the Jimi Hendrix Experience.) MacGraw, pretty as a picture—and the picture was *The Getaway*—liked my dogs. McQueen dug my attitude—and, evidently, what I was smoking. While she stroked the dogs, Steve and I smoked a doob, or what was left of it. With thumb and forefinger, he snuffed what was now a roach and said, "Where in this chichi town can a guy and his girl find a decent sandwich?"

I pointed to the sign on a one-story building across the street.

"Venice *Gourmet* Deli," he read. "The only 'gourmet' I dig is Eydie."

I laughed. "Don't let the G-word fool you. It's meant mainly for tourists. But the sandwiches are frou-frou-free."

He chuckled, and off we went. I handed Ali the reigns and she walked my two hounds across Bridgeway. Three splendid beauties, all three tall and slender, and from behind they had basically the same long, silky hairdo and smooth, springy gait—only two, though, had long curved tails. Ali, however, carried hers just as high.

While standing in the deli, waiting to order, Steve asked what sandwich I recommended.

"I heard you've got a reputation for being fearless," I replied, "so I say go with the pastrami."

He flashed that crinkly million-dollar grin—a ray of sunlight, like a cinematographer's Key-light, illuminated his icy blues. "And what are you getting, pal?"

"Me? Well, I'm chicken-shit," I said, "so I'm going with the chicken salad."

He laughed. You could tell Ali loved it when he laughed and liked that I was making him laugh. And I liked that she liked.

Okay. Yeah. Sure. He was a movie star. The biggest. But my

impression of the man is that in a world of fakery, he was the real McCoy. The real McCool. Probably didn't have a bogus bone in his body.

So, what was a real guy, a tough guy, a badass like McQueen doing in the mollycoddled world of Hollywood? Well, one look at Ali and one could only assume that acting was a great way to meet beautiful women.

* * *

EDWIN HEAVEN

1969
THE MISFORTUNES OF MISS FORMAGGIO

It all began when Elena Formaggio told her father—who, incidentally, was a South Philly cop—she was going away with girlfriends to a music festival in Upstate New York.

This I didn't know till we landed in Montego Bay.

"You lied to a cop?"

"He's old-school Italiano. He still treats me like his 'bella bambina,'" she said. "Only way he'd let me go off to Jamaica with a man was if we were man and wife. Telling a little fib was better than getting into a knock-down-drag-out fight."

Once outside the terminal, an airport cop came up to us. Since we weren't holding, we weren't the least uptight. After all, let's face it, bringing weed into Jamaica would be like bringing a soda cracker to a Roman banquet. He pointed out a couple locals loitering just down the road a ways. One had long dreads worn in a topknot, the other wore a striped Rasta cap. They couldn't be much older than twenty.

"Those two will try to sell you ganja," he said. "Execute caution."

Like an upstanding citizen (which I wasn't), I thanked the officer. Even complimented his black peaked cap with its red band. (Later, Elena would yank my chain saying I sounded just like Eddie Haskell, the well-known brown-noser. "Your cap looks lovely, Mrs. Cleaver," she gibed.)

As soon as the Jamaican cop walked away, we made a beeline for the ganja dealers.

Mere minutes later, we were in a tropical shantytown, among rows of rickety shacks. Theirs had a makeshift bar in the backyard. The pub table was basically a door painted red with a string of Christmas lights for ambiance.

"It's our likkle go-go club," said Rasta cap.

We smoked ganja and guzzled Red Stripe. The beer was warm, the weed powerful. A calm washed over us as Topknot played 45 RPMs. It was the first time I heard the word *reggae*. We had officially arrived in Jamaica.

I got so zonked, I was waiting for go-go dancers to appear.

Just before we parted, I scored a "likkle" bag of ganja. Didn't see the point of buying more since we'll be staying in Negril with a notorious grower.

They pocketed a Jamaican $20 banknote, each. I also tossed in a few extra bucks for the go-go dancers, if and when they happened to materialize.

"Praise Jah!" they said.

Not till we had driven off did it dawn on us: the airport cop was in cahoots. Why else would he specifically point out these dealers? Clearly, he was getting a kickback. I told Elena she should tell her dad about this Jamaican hustle, would be a cool way to increase his earnings, and she bopped me in the arm. For a bantamweight, she threw a right cross like Sonny Liston.

"We will never mention Jamaica to my dad," she said.

And we laughed like idiots. Stoned idiots.

That is, until Elena yawped, "Watch out! Crazy driver! Crazy driver!"

"Aye aye!" I said, swerving to avoid a head-on collision.

"I-yi-yi!" she said, making a sign of the cross and muttering a stream of Hail Marys.

We had to drive, me high to the hilt, all the way to Negril in a Morris Minor, the British auto Jamaicans called *fenkeh fenkeh.*

Which meant puny. It was like I was behind the wheel of a kiddie car. We were buckled up, of course, but wished the car had come equipped with crash helmets. The only route to South Negril was a narrow zigzagging single-track road. Two vehicles would rapidly approach one another, forcing one—the saner of the two—to pull over and allow the other passage.

Miraculously, we arrived in Negril, unscathed.

And, might I add, extraordinarily aroused.

Now hold that thought.

Tranquility Base, located at the southernmost part of Negril, was a well-kept secret. One of the previous occupants was "Beatle" George Harrison. One might call it a bed and breakfast, except it only had one guestroom. Its owner Dandy Connell (pronounced "Dondy") served breakfast at six a.m. consisting of freshly caught fish and fried plantain. Dondy, the perfect host, rolled giant spliffs for his guests, and we were pleasantly stoned our entire stay. At the time, this part of Negril was without electricity. Our room was lit by a kerosene lamp, which made the romantic nights even more romantic. Or, to put it another way, we fucked a whole lot.

Not going to bore you with overly ornate prose about how white the beaches were, how clear the blue waters, or how tropical the sun—you can read that in a travel brochure. What you probably won't read in a brochure is how sunburnt you can get. Ask Elena. When she removed her bikini top, that first day, she was red all over, except for her milky-white breasts. When naked, it made her look as if she was naked beneath her nakedness.

Dondy provided us with a bright twelve-year-old guide named Teddy. The night before, I taught little Teddy how to play checkers, and he became so obsessed with the game, he'd follow us around chanting, "King me, mon! King me!"

Dondy thought it especially wise to have a guide with us when we swam in the Caribbean, in the event one of us got stung by a conch—a venomous species of sea snail, its toxins possibly causing paralysis or death—and Teddy would be there to pee on it. (That's right, mon, pee.) I requested of Teddy that his bladder always held a sufficient supply of antidote. While Elena remained in the clear blue shallows, where she could see her feet and make certain she wasn't encroaching conch territory, I swam out toward the horizon and came to a peculiar spot in the sea where it was, once again, shallow enough that I could stand straight up. To a casual observer, it might appear as if I was walking on water. I could see my checkers protégé onshore and, pounding my chest like King Kong, yelled, "King me, Teddy, king me!"

Apparently, he thought I was shouting, "Help me, Teddy, *help me!*" Because, in no time flat, he came splashing up to me—his bladder full and his pubescent pecker at the ready.

Before you ask—yes, the urine cure was strictly Jamaican lore (although I didn't discover this fact till long after I was back in the States). Nonetheless, that didn't make Teddy any less a hero, at least in my book, and his tip was befitting one. Elena showed her gratitude by making him a paper crown to wear whenever he played checkers. And "King-Me-Teddy" was his moniker from thereon.

We partied on the beach that night, ate fresh-caught snapper grilled over a blazing twenty-gallon oil drum, and danced to a reggae band under a kazillion stars. Then, before an early bedtime—after all, a six a.m. breakfast rolls around rather quickly—we hung out on the porch with The Connells. Their house was all porch across the front, perfect for catching an ocean breeze and an intoxicating waft of star jasmine.

Dondy's age was pretty much imperceptible. Barring his snowy hair, he was lean and spry. My guess was that he was somewhere between fifty and seventy. Maybe. Since we arrived, he'd been calling me "Flynn," and I was curious as to why. So, I asked his wife. Mrs. Connell had a towering pouf of silver hair and liked wearing elegant Victorian dresses buttoned to the neck, even on the warmest nights. A black Scarlett O'Hara. She was a woman of great bearing and grace, or seemed to be, at least till she laughed, which was like a stevedore's—loud and hearty. The way she explained it—her husband calling me Flynn—had something to do with my mustache and how it reminded Dondy of his old friend, the dashing Errol Flynn, who had once lived on the island and moored his yacht off the coast of Port Antonio. Of course, I took the Errol Flynn comparison as a compliment, even though, days later, I found out that Flynn was what he called all mustachioed white men.

Elena asked Dondy if she resembled any movie star he might've had an acquaintance with. He scrunched his eyes and held up a lantern to get a better glimpse of her in the porch's semidarkness.

"Ya, mon," he said, beaming. "Nah-talie Wood."

Soon as he said it, I saw it, too. The brown, deep-set eyes, the indulgent smile and, by all means, the A-list boobies. Even in the semidarkness and her face being lobster red, I could still make out the blush on her cheeks.

That night in bed, I called her "Nah-talie." She called me Robin Hood. And we laughed our fool heads off—mighty fine ganja, Dondy—and probably woke all of Sherwood Forest.

The thing about Jamaica was its slow-motion pace. No one seemed to ever be in a hurry. Not once did I hear someone say, "Be right there!" Was always, "Me soon come." (Which we said to one another quite often at night, while in the sack.) But, even with its languid pace, the days flew by, and, before we knew it, we were in the Morris Minor zigzagging back to Montego Bay.

Before boarding our return flight to Philly, we spotted the same airport cop, the one who had handily pointed out the ganja dealers. I waved and mouthed a droll "thank you." He turned away, of course, acting as if he didn't know what I was inferring.

Our flight had a short layover in Miami, just long enough for a straggle of Philly-bound passengers to board. One such passenger had Elena ducking for cover.

"Oh, Jesus!" she said. "It's my aunt!"

What were the odds?

She nosedived into my lap and covered her head with an in-flight magazine.

"Oh God, we're in some deep shit! She sees me, she tells my dad!"

"What do you mean we're in deep shit? I wasn't the one who barefaced lied to him."

As the aunt made her way up the aisle, she seemed more determined to find a vacant seat than find her niece face down in some guy's lap and, like an ostrich, her head hidden.

Auntie, with that deep Miami tan and bottle blonde bouffant, could pass for a mobster's wife, though not half as dangerous as being a cop's sister.

When the seat belt sign was turned off, I shot a glance at the rear of the plane. Auntie looked like she was napping. I passed this along to Elena, suggesting she sit up, take a load off my groin. But not wanting to risk it, she hid under a magazine for the remainder of the flight.

I glanced back, after a while, and, oh shit! Auntie had decided to stretch her legs and was making her way down the aisle, toward us. When I relayed this distressing bit of news to Elena, she let out a muffled groan. Although I thought it impossible, she buried her head even deeper into my groin. To a passerby, it must've looked like, beneath that magazine, someone was performing fellatio.

There she was, just a few feet away, Elena's aunt. She stood there for what seemed like an eternity. Like something straight out of an Alfred Hitchcock thriller . . . *To Catch a Niece*. She was waiting for the stewardess to push the beverage trolley forward, but—thank goodness—decided to head back to her seat.

Though it was touch-and-go till we debarked in Philly, Elena managed miraculously to go undetected by her aunt.

She had dodged one bullet, but could she dodge another?

When we got to South Philly, I dropped her off a block from her house. It was her idea, not mine. If her father was still up, she was going to tell him her girlfriends dropped her off.

Not till days later did she fill me in on the details of the debacle.

The moment she stepped foot into the house, there he was, waiting for her, newspapers spread out on the coffee table.

"Well, *Miss Formaggio*," he said, "you decided to come home, finally." She told me he only called her that when he was about to bust her for some household infringement, and she thought it best to clam up and not say another word without a lawyer present. "So, tell me," he persisted, "how was the music festival? . . . 'Groovy?'"

If permitted one phone call, it would be to me to say, *Arrivederci, Googy*. She chose her words carefully. "Aw, dad, I had a tiring trip and really need to go straight to bed. G'night," and headed toward her bedroom.

"Not so fast," he said, holding up a newspaper, its mammoth front-page banner made her big brown eyes even bigger: 400,000 HIPPIES MIRED IN A SEA OF MUD, it read, accompanied by AP photos of muddy festivalgoers drenched by a downpour of biblical proportions. "Where the hell didja get that goddamn tan?"

All this, of course, took her by surprise, having, been out of touch with the world for days. To her utter horror, that obscure music fest in Upstate New York—the one she was supposed to go to with girlfriends—turned out to be none other than the biggest fucking event in music history. Woodstock!

The misfortunate Miss Formaggio had learned the hard way: there's no such thing as a "little" lie.

EDWIN HEAVEN

1976
BEING JACK

Once upon a line or two, I partied with Jack Nicholson.

It was an after-party for the San Francisco Film Festival that was hosted by psychedelic collagist Wilfred Sätty. It was held in his infamous basement, a decadent cavern decked out in deco and dolls— the creepy German bisque kind. Jack and I, however, lazed upstairs in the library on cushy 1920s shellback armchairs, chewing the fat with Francis Ford Coppola and Sätty's beauteous wife, Martha— who was all smiles. Psychedelics will almost always have that effect.

Francis and I were enjoying the company of a thousand books, while Jack enjoyed the company of quite a number of young women. He remained in the library for only short intervals. Parked out front was a Rolls Royce Silver Cloud where he'd, now and then, bring a stone fox and give her, shall we say, the private tour. The backseat was accessorized with Venetian blinds for privacy. After no more than twenty minutes, he'd return and we'd continue whatever conversation we were having. I venture to guess this dalliance occurred maybe three times while Francis and I were in the library, a different stone fox each time. It all looked so easy. He'd flash his signature toothy smile and arch his eyebrows in that devilish way of his and, like a powerful magnet, they were pulled across the room. Within minutes, they were in the Rolls getting the private tour.

After the third "tour," I said to him, "You must love being Jack Nicholson."

"Well," he said, spotting yet another beauty entering the room, "it sure as hell don't suck."

EDWIN HEAVEN

1962

THE WINDCIDENT

When I was seventeen, it turned out to be a very good year. I had moved in with my grandfather, a definite improvement over the previous year, that's because my father—drinking more than ever—was forever wrecking the house, and my nerves.

Like the night he was drunk out of his gourd, stumbling around in nothing but his boxer shorts, like a Jake Lamotta in search of a Sugar Ray, tearing the house apart painting by painting, book by book, all the time his fists clenched for battle and his pecker flapping in the breeze like the flag over Fort McHenry.

I loved my dad, don't get me wrong, he was brilliant and talented. Among his many skills was burping. He could burp the entire alphabet, and burping the letter W was no easy task. And, when he wasn't sloshed, was the sweetest, funniest, kindest man. But, this was a bad year for Dad, so, of course, I jumped at the chance to move in with Gramps.

There was never an inkling of tension in his home, just lots of love and homemade horseradish. The only thing we ever bickered about was wrestling. Not the collegiate kind—the professional kind.

Here was a man, born in Russia, who came to America believing that professional wrestling was for real.

"It's legit," he would argue, while munching on a pickled tomato.

"It's not, Gramps," I quibbled. "It's rehearsed and choreographed. Nothing but an exhibition. Funny, but phony."

"Faahh!" he responded, always insisting that it was the real thing, a gruesome clash, those knuckle-chops between the eyes, those wide-and-wild kicks to the groin—he believed every one of them landed with authority. Every one of them, every bit as real and extemporaneous as any Cousy jump shot, Koufax fastball or Unitas touchdown pass. Whenever I brought up the subject of some wrestling match being fixed, Gramps would respond with the usual "Faahh! What do you know? You don't know a karate chop from chop liver!"

But, aside from the issue of wrestling, ours was as grand a grandfather/grandson relationship as any. And to show my loving thanks, I gave him my favorite necktie. A paisley job, the color of mustard with only a few ketchup stains. I used to kid him and call it his "mustard-and-ketchup tie, hold the pickled tomato." He cherished it, that's for sure, and wore it every day. Ketchup stains and all. The red spots increased daily. It was how he expressed his love for me, I suppose.

Until "The Windcident."

I had coined that word shortly after the incident: the time I broke wind in my grandfather's face. That's right—farted in the kisser of my mother's good-hearted father. Now why would somebody go and do such a crass and imbecilic thing?

Well, for one, the crass seventeen-year-old imbecile that I was at the time thought it would be funny.

Earlier in the day, Benny Fishman had bent over, pointed to his rump, and asked me if there was a tear in his pants. When I inspected it, a bit too closely—brrraaappp! He farted right in my face. After the initial shock and malodorous aftermath, I laughed right along with Benny. So how was I to know that Gramps wouldn't laugh along with me? Aside from our running debate over professional wrestling, hadn't we laughed at all the same jokes?

"Hey, Gramps," I said, in between The Masked Marauder's bogus blows to Gorgeous George's kidneys. "Is there a tear in my pants?"

He had to tear his eyes from the tube to give the fictitious tear close inspection. Putting his nose inches from my buttocks, my grandfather gave a look-see. Then—brrraaappp!—I let one go.

He was so insulted by the flatulent assault, so utterly sunk by his daughter's son, he didn't even bother to say "Faahh!" He just walked away, steamed, right there in the middle of his esteemed wrestling show. And as he did, he tore off his tie.

Each passing day, it hurt more and more to see Gramps sans tie. My apologies seemed to fall on deaf ears. His eyes would glaze over, and I would become The Invisible Grandson.

And then, one miraculous night about three weeks after The Windcident, I sank a half-court buzzer-beater to sink Penn State Frosh. And the next morning, there was Gramps, proud as punch, with the sports section opened to my prodigious achievement, which he had circled neatly with a red ballpoint.

And there it dangled, mere inches below his magnificent grin: that glorious mustard-yellow tie. Every paisley seemed to be smiling. Even the little ketchup stains looked pleased.

From that day forward, never again did I break wind in my grandfather's presence—let alone, in his face. And every chance I got, I sat beside him on the sofa and watched professional wrestling on the tube. And I would cheer—yes, CHEER—right alongside him, for Gorgeous George to pin The Masked Marauder.

Even when I was certain it wasn't George's turn to win.

EDWIN HEAVEN

1973

LED SNIFFELIN

When rock impresario Bill Graham announced that Led Zeppelin would be headlining Kezar Stadium, it read on the poster: Supporting Acts to Be Announced.

For the Tubes, a virtually unknown band at the time, being one of the "supporting acts" was quite a big deal and probably would not have happened if not for the persistence of one Herbie Herbert, Journey's manager.

That sunny afternoon, as they performed their outrageousness to a capacity crowd of 50,000, I stood off stage alongside rock gods Jimmy Page and Robert Plant. Each had in hand their very own Vicks Sinex Nasal Spray, which frequented their respective nostrils.

Squirt-squirt, sniff-sniff.

Squirt-squirt, sniff-sniff.

After this went on for a while, I leaned in closer—but, not too close that I would catch germs—and said, "I take it you guys have colds?"

Well, they nearly bust a gut.

Jimmy, with that charming smile (and teeth whiter than any Brit rocker I'd ever met) snorted, "Don't think of us ungentlemanly. We'd offer you some, but you understand, it's been up our bleeding noses."

I laughed, realizing it wasn't the sniffles they had, just the sniff-sniffs. (Yes, back then I was still a bit innocent and naive.)

"Oh, definitely," I said, not without embarrassment. "I understand entirely."

And so, to this day—*ooh, it makes me wonder, ooh, it really makes me wonder*—just how good their dampened blow must've been.

* * *

THE NIGHT I GOT DAVID BOWIE LAID *sorta*

EDWIN HEAVEN

1956

UNHITTABLE

I asked my dad why he drank a lot, and he said it was to put out the fire in his arm—the bursitis.

Way before I was born, my dad (before he got into the ad game) played on a Detroit Tigers farm club. Weren't called Double-A or Triple-A back then. Nope, they were "farm clubs." Probably because the ballplayer worked his ass off like hayseeds, and got paid cow manure.

When Dad wasn't pitching, which he did about every three games, he was positioned in right field. Though he wasn't any good with a glove, he could knock the horsehide off a baseball. Those long throws he had to make from way out there in the distant pastures of right field weren't exactly the best "between starts" recovery routine for a pitcher. So, it wasn't long before that golden arm turned tin.

But, man, could he swing a bat.

In an exhibition against the "Negro League," as it was called once upon a crime, my dad batted against the great Satchel Paige, who many a prodigious hitter swore was unhittable. Dad dug his spikes deep into the furthest region of the batter's box, so deep in the box he almost spiked the catcher's toe. Evidently, he was looking fastball.

"Mr. Paige had two overpowering fastballs," said my dad, sipping a frosty Rolling Rock. "The supersonic 'Long Tommy' and the *unhittable* 'Little Tommy.' And to make it even harder on the hitter, he was the trickiest damn pitcher I ever stood in against."

As Dad explained it, he had that famous long, high kick. And those huge "clown" shoes the size of satchels. "But the trickiest trick of all was how Satchel Paige would shred the long sleeves he wore beneath the jersey, so his pitching motion looked like a wild, wind-blown May pole. Or ladies' nylons dangling on a clothesline in a March wind. Or a dozen dancing, wiggling sidewinder snakes. And somewhere among all this trickery was what appeared to be a pea traveling at 105 mph, directly toward your chinny-chin-chin."

Chin music, my dad called it. "Not exactly my favorite tune," he said.

Right out of the gate, Dad saw two "Long Tommies," then one "Little Tommy" and somehow—no easy task—managed to put the barrel on the ball. It was hard hit but hopped, skipped and jumped into the shortstop's tiny glove, and he was tossed out at first.

But he was "proud" of this at-bat, because Mr. Paige had fanned everybody else. They swung and hit nothing but cool Canadian air.

So, I suppose, to simply make *contact* off Paige was quite the accomplishment.

As Dad walked back from first base to the dugout, he heard what sounded like a smattering of applause. First, he thought it was from the grandstand, but then he looked over at the mighty man on the mound. Satchel was clapping. Dad had hit the unhittable.

"Sometimes, what seems like failure," my dad said, "turns out to be one of life's greatest triumphs."

Then he rubbed his aching shoulder and said, "Get me another Rolling Rock, son.

EDWIN HEAVEN

1987
SOMETHING FISHY ABOUT VERONICA

No nursery school today. Or tomorrow. Or, for that matter, the next day. It's summer and Audrey, my four-year-old daughter, was about to scale the apartment walls.

"Let's go for a drive," I said, shutting off the prehistoric typewriter. I figured I'd do what I've had to do all summer, try to write after I put her to bed. That's if I had any strength.

"Where to?" she asked, letting an armful of Barbies flop to the floor.

"I know a lake," I told her.

"What's the name?"

"Veronica," I said, for lack of a better name.

Later, of course, I find out it had another name. Lake Lagunitas.

But I was sure if Audrey knew, she'd still prefer Veronica.

When we arrived, a hearing-impaired park ranger informed us quite audibly that it was going to cost us three bucks just to drive through the gate.

"This lake better be good," I grumbled to myself, and dished out the three bucks, not unlike Jack Benny.

We then took a wiggly road for about a mile or so until we reached a parking area big enough for about three or four dozen cars. Except ours was the only one.

"Veronica won't win a popularity poll," I said, as we climb out of the car.

"Where is Veronica?" she asked, peering around at nothing but grassy slopes.

"I think Veronica's hiding from us," I said, equally befuddled, my feet heavy as logs.

As we stood there scratching our heads, and various mosquito bites, three small children suddenly alighted from a dark, nondescript van that seemed to have pulled up from out of nowhere, its dusty cloud a magician's puff of smoke.

The oldest of the children, a boy about eight, apparently with exceptional hearing, pointed us in the direction of the lake. "There ain't no Veronica over there, just old Lagunitas. And a whole lotta skeeters."

I gave a conspiratorial wink to the frazzled fellow getting out of the driver's side, and told the boy that Veronica Lake looked a darn sight better on a movie marquee. They both gave me a look as if I was playing Pinochle with a 52-card deck.

(Not to stray from the lake, but back when I was just a few years older than Audrey was at this time, my father had 86'd Veronica Lake from his nightclub on account of she was disturbingly drunk, and being that he knew I had a schoolboy crush on the beautiful movie star with the peekaboo hairdo, he broke the news to me gently as if he was telling me Peter Rabbit had been turned into a stew.)

Meanwhile, Audrey was getting along famously with the two young girls. And it didn't take long before we knew everyone's name.

The smallest was Brandy. She was the same age as Audrey, but about a head shorter.

Darlene was about six and had what looked like strawberry yogurt smeared all over her mouth and chin.

The boy was Ivan and sort of resembled the 1950s actor Aldo Ray, before Aldo Ray became mostly neck.

The frazzled fellow was Hank. He was their driver and counselor. The kids, I discovered, were from a "home" for abused children.

Audrey and I thanked them for the directions and started on

our hike up the grassy slope toward the elusive Veronica.

"What's a hike?" Audrey asked, never missing an opportunity to add a new word to her booming vocabulary.

"Walking outdoors," I replied, giving her soft, sticky hand a tender loving squeeze. "Over hill and dell." Suddenly I was cognizant of the fact that two years of single parenting had made me sound a little like Mother Goose.

We soon came upon a diagram of a fish.

"What's that?" Audrey wanted to know, pointing a plumpish little finger. It occured to me that if she were the fabled Gretel, the witch would already have the oven on pre-heat.

I told her it was a sign that told people where it was okay to fish. Then added, "Wanna fish?"

She wasn't sure, but nodded anyway. Her only perception of the sport was her macho Uncle Mikey's strange obsession with sharks. And, possibly, a Goofy cartoon. Either way, the thought probably made her more than a bit skittish.

Then, like a couple of loonies who forgot to take their mood stabilizers, Audrey and I went bounding along a dirt path the color of Orangina. It didn't take long before the path started to squirm around Veronica.

As lakes go, Veronica was no big thing. But we didn't care.

Right about now, we'd settle for an oversized puddle.

Lying in the path, as if it had grown tired of waiting and decided to take a little afternoon snooze, was a stick. Larger than a sprig, smaller than a bough. Just right for a fishing pole.

Further ahead, we found some tangled twine, which I patiently untangled and tied securely to the end of the stick. "A match made in heaven," I said to myself, pleased so far with the results of our impetuous search.

"What now?" asked Audrey. She was so excited, she was buzzing. Or maybe it was just a mosquito.

"What now?" said I, trying to memorize forever that smile on her face. "Now we keep our eyes peeled for a hook. Or even a safety pin."

Then, suddenly my persona transformed from that of Mother Goose to that of Coast Guard Chief Petty Officer "Poochy" Altman, my old boot camp drill instructor, and Audrey and I proceeded to march merrily around Veronica in mock military cadence.

"Go to your left your right your left, go to your left your right your left," I barked in an odd gung-ho warble. Sort of a mixture of Stan Laurel and Oliver North. "I gotta gal in Baltimore, hon-ney hon-ney, I gotta gal in Baltimore, bay-abe bay-abe."

We made up the lyrics as we tramped along—and, of course,

they were a lot cleaner than the ones I recalled emanating from the mouth of Poochy Altman. For instance, with Baltimore we rhymed big toy store. And so on.

Until we passed a family of fishermen by the name of Smith.

The Smiths smiled at the makeshift rod, which Audrey carried over a shoulder like an anorexic bazooka, and quipped good-naturedly about the sophistication of our equipment—or lack of—and how we probably stood as good a chance of catching a fish as they did.

"If they're out there, we'll catch them," I said, giving Audrey a nod of confidence. Then, dangling the naked line, I added, "That's if we can dig up something remotely resembling a hook."

Mr. Smith gave me the most agreeable grin I've seen outside of Andy Griffith reruns, and says, "I think The Smiths can do even better than that."

Whereas he reached carefully into a big metal box and took out a fancy-looking hook, which he tied to our line, then baited it with smelly salmon eggs.

"Caviar!" I told Audrey. "For you, nothing but the best."

We thanked The Smiths and off we went. Hook, line, and stinker.

We soon spotted Hank across the lake, swatting at the air. We assumed he was waving, so we waved back. The kids saw us and returned the wave. In no time we were all waving so deliriously we looked like the Signal Corps.

The moment we got to their fishing spot, I dropped Audrey's line into the lake and instructed her on what to do if it started to tug. "Hold on tight," I said. "And yell like crazy!"

Then I plopped down on a log next to an even-more-frazzled Hank. "You look pooped, Pop," he wheezed, slapping an ear so hard it soon turned cauliflower.

"Yeah," said I, catching my breath and a pesky mosquito at the same time. "But never too pooped to Pop!"

I'm afraid my play on words buzzed past him like just another close-range mosquito.

Bzzzt. Smack! Hank's ear was now the color of stinky salmon eggs.

I averted my attention from Hank's bloody onslaught and observed my daughter as she took a long, satisfying swig of spring water from a plastic container which Brandy held for her—while Audrey kept both hands firmly on the makeshift pole in case a shark should suddenly bite.

"Know what water does after you swallow it?" she said to Brandy, not unlike Huck Finn.

Brandy had no idea what it did, other than occasionally winding up in her underpants.

"It goes down to your toes and swiggles around and around and around." Audrey scientifically charted the water's route with her finger, which ended up circling the air an inch or so above her dusty red sneakers. Then, like some pint-sized anatomy professor, she added, "And then it goes back up, up, up . . . and OUT!" Her finger charted the return trip very graphically.

Poor little Brandy took this all in as any four-year-old would who had just been informed of the unwonted fact that her toes were, in actuality, bladders. In other words, bug-eyed and slack jawed. I noticed, from that point on, she sort of walked on her heels.

Ivan, meanwhile, was having a whopping good time casting his line into the lake—about every twenty seconds.

"Careful!" shouted Hank, between swats. "Hold that hook away from the kids!"

All this time, Darlene was doing a ravenous job on a large bag of barbeque potato chips. Hank was worried that she was eating too many and might get sick. Again.

I was then informed by Hank that she had been carsick several times earlier—and suddenly it dawned upon me that the pinkish smear around her mouth wasn't strawberry yogurt after all.

Darlene had a great laugh which revealed several missing front teeth—a normal sight for someone her age—but, nevertheless, the fact that she was an abused child haunted me, and I silently prayed that she had lost those tiny teeth the natural, nonviolent way. I was also thinking that if I were the tooth fairy, Darlene would be rolling in enough coin to buy a ton of chips.

"Only thing bitin' 'round here is these dang skeeters!" said Ivan, with more than a hint of disgruntlement.

"How would you know," said Hank. "You don't leave your hook in long enough to give a poor fish time to open its mouth!"

"I gotta nibble!" giggled Audrey, holding up a partially devoured salmon egg as proof.

"Way to go, darling!" I said, and gave her a congratulatory high-five.

Before we know it, it was time to leave. Which had never been Audrey's favorite time.

Sadly, she hugged her new friends goodbye. Then, as we were turning to leave, she asked Brandy, "Wanna play with me again?"

Brandy nodded yes, about six or seven times. And the two of them did a cute little dance—Brandy was being very careful, though, not to put too much weight on her ten little bladders.

Then, like a little adult, Audrey told Brandy to give me a phone number.

"No can do," interjected Hank, and added apologetically, "against the rules."

Audrey and Brandy had identical pouts.

Hank conceded a little. "Give me your number, Ed," he said. "If I get approval, maybe we can arrange a place for the kids to meet. You know, a park or something." Then chuckled, "Some place where there's no mosquitoes."

I gave him our number and told him I hoped they'll call.

Then Audrey and I waved farewell to Veronica Lake, as if it were a dear old friend departing for Timbuktu.

Climbing the embankment, Audrey slipped and scraped her knee. She started to cry a little, trying her best to hold back the tears, and that's when Darlene scampered over like a big sister and tried to comfort Audrey by saying, soothingly, "Don't cry, Audrey, don't cry. Your daddy loves you—at least your daddy loves you."

I'm choked and must look away, because when it came to holding back the tears, I was having an even harder time than a four-year-old with a scraped knee.

On the way home we stopped off in Mill Valley at Captain Video. I was in the mood for something like *I Married A Witch* starring none other than our favorite Lake. But it was Audrey who had the best idea of all. She wanted to watch *Oliver!* A movie about an abused child—who lived happily ever after.

Three bucks well spent.

EDWIN HEAVEN

1974

TERI BANANA

Before *Young Frankenstein*, there was a Dole banana.

In fact, you might say it was I who discovered Teri Garr, not Mel Brooks—if not for the fact that she had already appeared as a dancer in a half dozen Elvis Presley films and had landed roles on a number of TV shows (including a *Star Trek* episode) before neither Mel or I laid eyes on her.

I had written a round of fifteen-second Dole banana TV commercials, and she was, at the time, just another one of many who auditioned.

The script called for a ditzy blonde to walk down a hall, stop at a vending machine, drop a coin, and pull a lever. Not exactly Lady Macbeth.

The kicker is: instead of the expected candy bar, out tumbles a banana.

"A banana!" exclaims Ditzy.

A voiceover says: "A Dole banana. As a snack, it's a natural."

Then we hear Ditzy's tinkling laugh.

Well, the art director, Brian McCarthy, and I had seen just about every "ditzy blonde" in Hollywood—of which there were many, some quite famous—but, this unknown actress (at least unknown to me) named Teri Garr was so funny and alluring, it didn't matter that she might not have been the prettiest. She was what I call "Goldie Hawn cute," had a ton of personality and, as far as I was concerned, perfect for the part.

But it was a different ball of wax for the client, Castle & Cooke. They wanted Louisa Moritz, the hottest, sexiest, ditsiest blonde in town. She had recently been featured in an American Motors commercial and was hilarious as the stereotypical dumb blonde. Not to mention her distinctive squeaky voice and comedic timing.

"Watch out for the *bus!*" shouts the nervous wreck of a driving instructor.

"*What* bus?" she squeaks.

"Behind the *truck!*" he screams.

"*What* truck?" she squeals.

It was one of my all-time favorite commercials. If not for having auditioned Teri, I would've jumped at the chance of working with Louisa. The client really wanted her. But, Brian and I wanted a fresh face and knowing that Teri brought more to the part than just ditz, we fought for her, tooth and manicured nail.

It wasn't quite The Rumble in The Jungle or The Thrilla in Manilla, but that night over dinner with the client it got mighty close to it—a battle of wills, as they say—and when the dust (and grated parmesan cheese) cleared, the part was Teri's. (And, miraculously, Brian and I hadn't lost our jobs!)

Oh, that Teri Garr hip shimmy! Oh, that smile! That special way she rolled her eyes! That tinkling laugh! Teri knocked it outta the park. And the rest is cinema history.

"A banana!"

Maybe it was just incidental, but shortly after the spot aired nationally, her career seemed to skyrocket. She landed one boffo film role after another. *The Conversation, Young Frankenstein, Mr. Mom, Close Encounters of the Third Kind, Tootsie, Oh, God!* and *The Black Stallion.*

It's debatable, I admit. Maybe I discovered her, maybe I didn't. In retrospect, more than likely I didn't. Her career might've already picked up steam before she sashayed into our casting session. But, hey, who knows? Maybe somewhere, Teri is telling someone she discovered me.

Although chances of that, I'd say, are slim.

Cue: tinkling laugh.

Directing Ms. Garr
© Edwin Heaven

EDWIN HEAVEN

1966

TRAPPED IN AN ELEVATOR
WITH JOEY HEATHERTON

Back when vinyl was small with a big hole in the middle and turntables turned forty-five times a minute, and even though I was still wet behind the ears, I fell in with the big time—a talented crop of Philadelphians churning out hit after hit. Songwriters and record producers like John Madara ("You Don't Own Me", "1-2-3", "At The Hop", "Rock And Roll Is Here To Stay", etc.), Leon Huff, who by stomping a pedal on an old upright piano could get an amazing bass drum effect ("Back Stabbers", "Expressway To Your Heart", "Love Train", "Me and Mrs. Jones", "Only The Strong Survive", "Use Ta Be My Girl", etc.), and Joe Renzetti, who scored the arrangements of many a hit including "Sunny", "98.6", and "Mandy" and would one day win an Academy Award for *The Buddy Holly Story*. No slouch, he.

Joe was one of those jolly guys who would still be jolly even if he were a beanpole, which he was not. He wore glasses with thick black bebop frames and always looked like the coolest cat in the room. The walls and ceiling of Joe's basement was lined with empty egg cartons, and I imagined there must be somewhere in his West Philly house another room jammed full of loose eggs delicately piled high to the ceiling. Whenever Joe and I would get together we'd spend most of the time just yucking it up. We thought each other funnier than hells bells. We also tossed ideas around. Like a comedic TV show not unlike Ernie Kovacs' but with weird people lip-syncing the hits. (This was long before there was such a thing as a TikTok.)

So, one day I walked into Madara's office with a little something Joe and I had written called "To Fernanda with Luv." It wasn't a catchy tune but could most definitely catch on. Its nonstop hilarity was a precursor to what would later be Rowan & Martin's hit TV show *Laugh-In*, a laugh every ten seconds. Well, Johnny flipped over it and gave us the green light to produce. Gave us studio time at Cameo-Parkway from midnight to morning. Even threw in future Rock & Roll Hall of Fame engineer Joe Tarsia. Madara, who resembled Marcello Mastroianni, had been a teenage heartthrob and permitted us to use a song he recorded and didn't mind at all when we lampooned it. "Be My Girl" had a hook—*I love you so madly, be my girl*—which we milked. Intercutting it throughout. At the very end, we (mercifully) fired gunshots—*blam blam blam*—till the refrain slowly died away. *I love you so maaaaaaaad—BLAM!* The record closes with footsteps fading and a door slamming. It was a rapid-fire, rat-a-tat-tat gag fest. Shtick after shtick after shtick.

For example, Sheri, a go-go dancer on the popular Hy Lit Show—who I was dating at the time, along with the show's other go-go dancer Susan (it was the Swinging Sixties, after all)—had this cute little voice that sounded like she was swigging helium and says, "Oh, I've been asked to get married lots of times."

A guy who sounds like Norton, Ralph Kramden's upstairs neighbor, says, "Oh yeah? Who'd ever ask you!"

"My mother, my father, my brother, my Uncle Charlie (fade). . ."

Police siren segues to *I love you so madly, be my girl!*

Cut to a Hammond organ (the soap opera kind) as a lovesick lad says, "Fernanda, I ain't gotta lotta money or a big house or two cars like Harry Winokour but I *love* you."

"I like you too," replies Fernanda, "but tell me more about . . . *Harry Winokour.*"

Organ crescendo, then cut to I *love you so madly, be my girl!* And so it went.

It would be an act of futility to try and put all two minutes and forty-eight seconds of lunacy on paper, for it was strictly an auditory experience. To fully appreciate "To Fernanda with Luv" you'd need to lend an ear (as Shakespeare so aptly put it).

We called ourselves Googy & Joe's Workshop, and the workshop turned out to be quite a piece of work. Especially considering back then in the old analog days of recording, it was all pieced together—all ninety-three edits—with a razor blade and adhesive splicing tape. Tarsia once told me he loved engineering this session more than any other, which is quite the commendation when you take into consideration that he engineered the likes of Gladys Knight, Dusty Springfield, The O'Jays, Harold Melvin & The Blue Notes, The Spinners, The Delfonics, Todd Rundgren and, oh yeah, David Bowie!

Okay, so "Fern" is released as a "DJ Copy Not For Sale" and—bang!—*Billboard* magazine is all over it, gives it their coveted "Best Bet" which leads to it getting a ton of airplay in a dozen markets. I started window-shopping XKEs and Joe stayed close to a phone in the event Ed Sullivan called.

But it was not to be.

Allen Klein (yes, the same Allen Klein who would one day break up the Beatles) bought Cameo Parkway. Not a record got shipped. End of story.

Well, not exactly.

I can't walk away from Cameo without first telling you of the time I got trapped in its elevator with a sex symbol.

Joey Heatherton was the sexiest little blonde in these here United States—as well as Vietnam if you're counting her many USO tours with Bob Hope.

If you're not of a certain age, you may not know her by name. But there's a mighty good chance you'll recognize that Tinker Bell face, that lithe hourglass figure, that short, sassy Sassoon hairdo, and those incredible dance moves. Back then, there were a bunch of variety shows and turn on the old boob tube and you'd probably see Joey Heatherton, a frequent guest on Bob Hope's show, Dean Martin's, Sonny & Cher's and especially Johnny Carson's. On one particular *Tonight Show*, little Joey showed Johnny how to do The Frug and on that night, I imagine fifty million eyeballs popped and twenty-five million jaws fell slack and few, very few, fell asleep in front of their TV. Sounds like I'm exaggerating, and I probably am, but not by much. To put it mildly, sexy-as-all-hell Joey could effing dance.

And on one night, she and I danced right onto an elevator. The show-off that I was, I did one of those Jackie Wilson spins. She did what looked like The Wah-Watusi combined within a little Pony stutter step. We laughed all the way to the ground floor, right up to the moment the elevator door wouldn't open.

I could think of a worse fate than being trapped in an elevator with super cute, super sexy Joey Heatherton. Making out, of course, was out of the question, she being engaged to my good friend John Madara.

But things got out of hand in a different way.

The jammed elevator door had a porthole overlooking busy Broad Street—one that passersby could peer into. We assumed this was to our advantage, so Joey and I banged our fists on that little round window hoping to draw the attention of someone passing by, get them to peer into the elevator see two people trapped inside and get somebody to open the damn jammed door. And peer into the elevator they did. Peer was an understatement. They gawked. Some pointed and laughed at our predicament.

"Look! It's Joey Heatherton!"

Others wolf-whistled or threw kisses. You see, Joey was so famous everyone probably thought it had to be some kind of TV gag. You know, like they were on Candid Camera. They probably wondered, Where's *Allen Funt?*

Seeing that no one was coming to our rescue, we said, "Fuck it! If it's a show they want, a show we'll give 'em," and with devil-may-care, did a corny tango around the elevator, moving forward, backward, sideways in what little space we had, while I hummed "La Cumparsita" like Jack Lemmon in *Some Like It Hot*—it being the only tango music I knew—and I admit I got a little carried away and took Joey by her trim waist and, as I pictured "The Latin Lover" himself, Rudolph Valentino, I placed a hand on her svelte upper back (yes, I svelte her up) and gently lowered her backward. As we dipped, she threw her head back, extending her supple nape and things started to get a little steamy, including the porthole window, and for a fleeting moment I put out of mind the crowd staring, as well as the fact she was betrothed to my goombah and, and… oh shit!

That's when the door decides to open.

We plowed through the crowd to a smattering of applause and race out into the middle of Broad Street and—get this—Joey hailed a *bus*! Like it was a giant taxicab! *And*—get this—right there in the middle of Broad Street it screeched to a stop to pick her up. The driver, clearly smitten, drove with one eye on the road, the other on Joey who crouched beside him. Then, after no more than a block or so, Joey said, "Right here is fine, thank you." And right there the bus pulled over like a limo, dropping us off right in front of a cocktail lounge.

Once inside, it wasn't very difficult getting the bartender's attention and Joey orders us drinks. "Two Singapore Slings," she said. And added that she was fond of maraschino cherries. When the drinks arrived, there were at least a half dozen cherries in her highball glass. Mine, of course, had not a single one. But who cares? I had Joey.

That is, until her fiancé joined us later.

Joey Heatherton and fiancé
Photo by permission of John Madara

* * *

EDWIN HEAVEN

2005
GLOBES AND GERMOPHOBES

The red carpet is the length of three football fields. Or so I'm told. The woman I'm standing next to is awesome but not what you'd call Hollywood glamorous. She isn't wearing Versace or Yves Saint Laurent. She's not wearing Harry Winston jewelry. Fact is, she's not wearing any jewelry. Unless you consider an FBI badge jewelry. She has long dark hair pulled back in a J.Lo ponytail. Her hazel eyes scan the crowd. No longer is it a game of *Where's Waldo?*—it's now *Where's Bin Laden?* With its FBI presence, the Hollywood Foreign Press is taking extra precaution the awards go off without a hitch. Or abduction. Rumor has it there's an al-Qaeda plot to kidnap Russell Crowe. I chuckle at the thought of a tuxedoed Crowe, in a gladiator's stance, legs-apart, wielding a short sword and weighted net.

Though not as imposing as an FBI badge, I am equipped with the proper credentials: a lanyard with an E! Network VIP Access Pass. Just about everywhere I look I see dolled up starlets, easy on the eyes all of them, but not one can stack up to Special Agent Awesome. Being a longtime sufferer of chronic impetuosity, I tell her this. She flushes and mutters what sounds like pshaw. In spite of a shy side, I can easily picture her using a battering ram to force open an evil-doer's door.

And I'm struck with an idea for a film. *FBI Babe.* Title role: Jennifer Lopez—in a ponytail.

My train of thought is abruptly derailed when, at the far end of the red carpet, there's a loud outburst. Agent Awesome doesn't reach into her concealed carry holster and whip out a firearm, though. It's not that kind of outburst. It's a booming ovation and it's just outside our field of vision, so I have no idea who or what it's for. Most likely, some hotshot movie star or rock god, and it's loud and sustained and totally nutso: screaming, yelling, shouting, wild applause, piercing whistles.

"Sounds like some rocker's gettin' a whole lotta love," I say.

"Led Zeppelin?" she says, as if hoping.

"Prince, I think," I say, seeing The Purple One heading our way.

He gets a nice round of applause, but it's nearly drowned out by the jacked-up, crazy shit at the far end of the carpet.

Not unlike the comic book hero Plastic Man, I crane my neck to catch a glimpse without my stepping on the red carpet, and I see Jagger approaching and I'm wondering if it's for Mick everyone's going bonkers. But like Prince before him, he gets a nice hand but the resounding ballyhoo at the red carpet's entryway drowns out the lion's share of his ovation.

"I think Mick just waved at you," I say to her.

"Looks like he's waving at you."

Unsure, we both wave back.

Meanwhile, the hooting and hollering continues at the far end. Whoever it is, sounds like he or she is walking on water. The cheers grow louder, crazier and closer, till, finally, we see who it is.

Taking long strides and walking tall, it's Quentin Tarantino and Uma Thurman.

The mad cheering dies down the moment they disappear into the Beverly Hilton International Ballroom.

"Royale with cheese," she says with a grin.

And with just those three words, she nails the whole Golden Globes mishegaas. And it comes to me—the tagline for *FBI Babe:* "She's quick, she's hot, she's packing heat."

Before taking my leave (a full bladder can be most insistent) I tell her it was a pleasure hanging with her.

"Likewise," she says, and gives me what I imagine to be her off-duty smile. "Maybe next year I see you on the red carpet."

"It's a date," I say.

Pshaw, she says.

In a rush to get to the ballroom and find a men's room, I take the red carpet route. It's quicker, more direct. I figure who's going to stop me? Not the FBI or the fashion police. Right before I step inside, I look back—but she's gone. Maybe raced off to snag a terrorist. (Perhaps the one hot on the heels of Russell Crowe.) Or, possibly, she vacated her station to hunt down a quarter-pounder.

A Royale with *pshaw*.

* * *

By now, my teeth are floating, as they say, like they're little white duckies bobbing about on the surface of a tidal bulge, and I speed-walk through various foyers—destination: the backstage men's room—and, as I do, I recall the maddest of mad dashes.

I had produced a trailer for the Mill Valley Film Festival and MVFF founder Mark Fishkin introduced me to Jim Jarmusch, the indie director of *Stranger Than Paradise*. He had a thick hank of snow-white hair cut asymmetrically that could've been styled by Nefertiti or Link Wray. It was already as iconic as Andy Warhol's—except Jim's head of hair wasn't a silver-gray wig. While we relaxed on a lobby sofa, an enthusiastic capacity crowd was already seated in the theater. It was the much-anticipated opening night screening of his newest work *Down by Law* and we drank beers while shooting the shit.Thenthelobbylightsdimmed,asignthatthefilm wasaboutto begin. Jim wisely put aside his beer, but I (unwisely) chug-a-lugged mine—which I would soon regret. The festival powers-that-be seatedmeintheaisleseatrightbesideJim's.Hisfilm (IlaterfoundJim's out) was not a long one, only about an hour and a half, yet on a bladder about to burst it felt as long as (a black and white) *Gone with the Wind*. (*Darn you, Coors!*) Midway into the film not only were my teeth floating (as they say), but they were also doing the Australian crawl! (*Please, please be an intermission*, I'm silently pleading.) I became all squirrelly in my seat, like I had ants crawling up my ass, squirmier than a toddler straining to hold it in. Sitting next to me must've been distracting. But I couldn't just leave my seat and race to the men's room. I was afraid the filmmaker might take it personally, get the impression I wasn't enjoying his film. (Which I surely would've had I emptied my bladder.) What a dilemma. Reminded me of that song by The Clash. *Should I stay or should I go now?* And I had to go!

Now! (There should be a film school rule that states: At a premiere, empty bladder before sitting next to its director.)

"Great film!" I told the director as the closing credits crawled, and was off like a shot, sprinting up the aisle to the nearest urinal. I don't think I ever ran quite that fast before or since. And when I finished peeing, the entire County of Marin must've heard my sigh of relief.

But I digress.

I finally reach my backstage destination and as I charge into the men's room, already undoing my fly, I see there are just three urinals. But, luckily, there's one unoccupied. The one in the middle. As I do my business, I give a sideways glance to my left and notice that the gent taking a leak next to me is a sixty-something tuxedoed version of Clyde Barrow. Oh wait, that's Warren Beatty! Then I do a sideway glance to my right and—holy *Mean Streets!*—it's Martin Scorsese!

Of course, I straightaway look straight ahead and act like taking a piss between two Hollywood legends is an everyday occurrence—and hailing from San Francisco, it certainly isn't.

Not a word is spoken. After all, pitching while piddling is uncouth. It's a lavatory, not an elevator. While we're pissing, a couple of things cross my mind. Like, how the three of us tinkling in unison sounds like a Vegas water show. The Fountains of Bellagio. And, which of these gentlemen had asparagus for lunch?

Then somehow, we finish at the same time and, together, shake off the last drop—which is when I decide to break the silence. "The Shakers!" I say.

The Hollywood legend to my right chuckles, "Not a bad name for a band."

Grins the Hollywood legend to my left, "A pissy band."

And laughing, The Shakers exit the men's room.

* * *

I should note that Warren Beatty dated a certain girlfriend of mine. Even though Warren supposedly slept with over 13,000 women (according to a biographer) I doubt he wouldn't recall her. But here at The Golden Globes was not the time for Warren to discuss a woman other than his lovely wife, who, presently, is standing within earshot, holding her Golden Globe a lot better, it seems, than she's holding her bubbly.

I must say this about the trophy in Annette's hand, it's smaller in-person than it appears on television and if it held batteries it might make some woman a fine sex toy.

It's apparent Annette has been celebrating for quite a while, and deservedly so, and is, shall we say, delightfully tipsy. In fact, the force of her jubilation nearly knocks my Throx off—which are socks that come in threes, so when you lose one you'll still have a pair. (A fashionable little invention of mine that found its way into celebrity gift bags.)

I look over at Warren and he shrugs, as if to say, *Hey, whadaya gonna do? Girls just wanna have fun.* And I'm thinking, *Yeah, 'specially if she just won Best Actress in a Comedy or Musical.* Warren, the supportive husband, seems content to give the wife center stage, and she can rock it all night long if she so pleases. After all, tonight they have a babysitter!

I glance to my right and there, once again, is Martin Scorsese. This time, however, he's not standing at a urinal. He and Leonardo DiCaprio are finishing up an E! interview. I drape a Kleenex over the palm of my right hand and extend it as the Golden Globe Winner for Best Actor in a Drama Motion Picture is walking in my direction.

"Congratulations, *Mr. Hughes*," I say.

Leo laughs and shakes the tissue-shrouded hand. It's an inside joke and having portrayed the billionaire germaphobic, he gets it.

In way of introduction, I say, "I'm Edwin Heaven."

His blue eyes go wide. "You're Audrey's dad?"

Now my eyes go wide. I'm surprised and not surprised. My daughter—a Sofia Coppola discovery—is more than likely right in the thick of the Hollywood scene.

"The one and only," I reply.

Leo, a proper gentleman, asks if I've met Martin Scorsese. Martin and I shake and, as we do, I say, "Yeah. If I recall, we shook before." Martin chuckles.

Before I can extract a tidbit about my daughter, their publicist drags him and Martin off to another interview. As he's leaving, he says, "Please, tell Audrey I said hello."   .

I waste little time and whip out my Nokia flip phone and dial up the kid.

"Hey, you," I say when she answers.

"Hey, Dad," she says. All around me is much celebration. "Where are you?"

"I'm here at the Golden Globes."

"Cool. Having fun, I hope?"

"Totally." Then, pausing for effect, I tell her Leo says hello, and all about our shaking Kleenex cloaked hands à la Howard Hughes. She laughs. Her laughter is perhaps my favorite sound.

The deliriously happy Annette Bening leans on my shoulder, acts like she's eavesdropping.

"Wanna say hi?" I ask.

"Who am I saying hi to?

"My daughter Audrey."

Into the phone she says, "Hi, daughter Audrey!"

I look over at Warren and he's happy she's happy. Those who know him know he's never been one to be led around by the nose but when Annette returns and leads him away like her tamed tiger, he doesn't mind in the least.

"Who was that?" Audrey asks.

"Oh, nobody special," I replied, matter-of-factly. "Just Annette Bening."

"Get *out!*" says Audrey and laughs. (Like I said, I love that laugh.)

We make plans to meet poolside the next day and before we hang up we say our goodbyes the way we usually say our goodbyes.

"I love my kid." I say.

"I love my dad," she says.

I notice the vivacious Glenn Close, resplendent in black and gold—black being the low-cut laced gown and gold being the trophy she's clutching—and she notices me noticing her and glides over.

"Wow," she says, her mood effervescent. "Where have *you* been hiding?" She emphasizes the pronoun.

"Not from you, my dear, that's for certain," I say, also emphasizing the pronoun.

Is she merely being affable and open (and by "open" I'm not just referring to the low-cut gown) or is she clearly coming on to me? *I should be so lucky*, I'm thinking. But then it comes to mind the haunting image from *Fatal Attraction* of that pet rabbit boiled alive and not wanting to wind up in a stew. Perhaps "hiding" isn't such a bad idea. I'm also wondering if a similar off-putting reaction befalls other actors like Anthony Hopkins (Hannibal Lecter) and Bella Lugosi (Count Dracula).

Suddenly people step aside, opening a clear lane for Clint Eastwood. And, talk about your celebrity overload, walking beside him is the Million Dollar Baby herself, Hilary Swank. Of all the bright smiles brightening this night, hers is by far the brightest. It outshines a roomful of Golden Globes. *It's the smile of a saint*, I'm thinking—that's *if* saints sashayed around in sleek copper-brown Calvin Klein satin gowns. Soon as the opportunity arises, I tell her what I was thinking: how she exudes a saintly aura like a beautiful, glamorous Mother Teresa. (These words may appear inane on paper but rolling off the tongue sounded sublime.)

"Oh my gosh!" she says, and we lock eyes. "That's the nicest compliment ever!"

I'm melting, but before I'm a puddle, Clint ("unforgivably") ushers Hilary to their next post-awards interview. As he leads her away, she glances back at me. "I really mean that," she says.

Me, too, I mouthed.

"Think quick!" says Jamie Foxx, tossing me a Kodak pocket Instamatic so I can take a picture of him and Giovanni The Margarita King. Jamie, who played Ray Charles, is holding his Golden Globe for Best Actor In A Musical or Comedy.

"Think quick!" I say, tossing the camera back at him, which he bobbles and drops.

"Hey, I didn't see that," he says.

"Ray wouldn't have, either," I say, "but I bet he would've caught it."

He exits laughing.

An hour later, I'm standing outside the Beverly Hilton, when Jennifer Coolidge, the beautiful, bosomy actress, asks what it is I'm holding. "Some kind of award?

I laugh. "It's a premium margarita in a bottle. The Margarita King. Here," I say, handing it to her like I'm a presenter and it's, indeed, an award.

She reacts as if it is, and thanks me, thanks her agent and thanks manager. It was quite funny.

"We can pop the cork right now," I say.

"Ooh, that sounds nasty."

We have a laugh. She says she has to get up at 5:30, which is just four hours from now.

Her stretch arrives. We say night-night. And as the limo slowly pulls away, she holds the bottle out the window and says, "Adiós mi amor!"

I floated all the way back to my hotel room.

Next day, I'm still floating. Except it's in a pool, and am inside an oversized Flamingo-pink inner tube, upon which rides little Harley girl, a year-old teacup Yorkie.

Poolside, the handsome English bloke lounging in the chair next to mine had offered to take a picture using my camera of Harley and me in the pool. To this day, it's among my very favorite photos. Turns out, this gentleman is an actor. But isn't almost everyone in this town? When he inquires, I tell him I'm a screenwriter. But isn't almost everyone in this town?

He asks if I'm working on anything right now.

"Randy, Rudy and Rose," I tell him.

What's it about, he wants to know. So I tell him and he tells me he loves it. So we exchange email addresses.

My daughter arrives. She's taking me to see a movie she saw the day before and says she can't wait to see it again with her dad. Says it's now her favorite all-time Christmas movie. "It's called *Love Actually*," she says. And then, noticing the guy lounging next to me, says to him, "You were great in it."

Turns out the bloke is Andrew Lincoln who plays Mark in *Love Actually* and who, in an iconic scene, stands outside Keira Knightley's front door and, as he plays "Silent Night" on a boombox, confesses his love using a stack of cue cards with phrases like "TO ME, YOU ARE PERFECT."

Later that afternoon, we saw the film and now, as a holiday tradition, watch it every Christmas.

So yes, I had randomly "pitched" someone whom I had no idea was the talk of the town. And—surprise, surprise—we weren't standing side by side at a urinal.

Photo snapped by Andrew Lincoln © Edwin Heaven, 2005

* * *

THE NIGHT I GOT DAVID BOWIE LAID *sorta*

EDWIN HEAVEN

1955
THE DAY I BECAME A MAN

Dad was an atheist. God existed only when somebody sneezed.

"God bless you," he'd say.

Or, if he banged a thumb while driving a nail.

"Goddammit!" he'd say.

But then, he'd say he was an agnostic on account of atheists don't get to celebrate holidays. And, oh boy, did Dad ever love to celebrate!

Naturally, being an adman, he was rooted in holiday commercialism. The fact is, we had the biggest Christmas tree on the block.

He perpetrated the myth of Santa when one Christmas Eve he staggered home from an office party in a Santa outfit and, with a merry ho-ho-ho, woke his two boys who sprang from their beds to sneak a peek at a jolly old elf placing gifts under the family's prodigious tree. Of course, I, being the youngest, failed to notice that instead of a stump of a pipe held tight in Santa's teeth, it was a Viceroy cigarette, the brand with "the thinking man's filter."

So, it shouldn't come as a surprise, then, that the extent of my Judaism was grandma's gefilte fish, a dish that looked gross yet, somehow, tasted divine when topped with her homemade horseradish. But, I didn't know Purim from Pesach, Rosh Hashanah from Yom Kippur, and had never twiddled with a dreidel.

I once saw a menorah in a neighbor's window and asked my dad what it was and he said, "They must be celebrating Liberace's birthday." (Liberace, of course, being the glitzy guy on TV with the incessant smile, a headful of wavy hair and always—on the lid of his grand piano—a candelabra.)

As age thirteen approached, suddenly came the unpleasant news that (and only out of respect for my grandparents) I was going to have a bar mitzvah.

"A bar what?"

Up until then, the only bars I knew were the ones my mom sent me to, to drag home my dad.

"A bar *mitzvah* turns a boy into a man," Mom said.

"Can't I just grow a mustache or get a tattoo?"

"Relax, kiddo," Dad said. "You get up there, recite a few goofy prayers and, voilà! The money comes pouring in!"

Easier said than done, because never had I faced a task so daunting or a language so incomprehensible. I was expected to chant something called the maftir, from something called the Torah, and then I'd have to sing—yes, *sing!*—something called the Haftorah. And do it all in Hebrew! Might as well have told me to sing it in Martian! It would be easier for a Sumo wrestler to climb Mt. Everest than for a Jew raised as a non-Jew (or, more precisely, as an agnostic) to pull off such an improbable feat, and do it, mind you, in like three month's time. Even if I was given a whole year, I probably couldn't do it. It took me that long to learn Pig Latin. A linguaphile I wasn't.

I tried, though. Oh Lord, did I ever. Sacrificing my nightly television time—missed a dozen episodes of The Honeymooners— talk about your child abuse. And every day right after school, instead of playing sandlot baseball, I had to take a bus across town to an ancient synagogue with a name I couldn't even pronounce— Shaareil Tfiloh—and spend hours with a doubly ancient orthodox cantor with herring-breath and a very short fuse.

Egods! Like I said, I tried my best, but best was not good enough.

It was no easy task learning a mysterious, otherworldly language, one that required me to read from right to left and use an alphabet with characters that looked more like wiggly musical notes.

Then, the dreaded day arrived and as the rabbi unrolled the Torah, I stood there on the synagogue podium, frozen with fear, gaping at a packed congregation. Relatives, many having traveled hundreds of miles. Neighbors, including Eugene "The Menorah Kid" who lived next door. My four-year-old sister Nan, who thought the sun shined out of my ass. My protective big brother Buddy, ready to punch anyone who dared to ridicule me. My mom, who that day resembled Ava Gardner more than ever. Some of Dad's business associates were there and already three sheets to the wind. Not to mention, a sea of rocking and praying Hasidic Jews. Come Shabbat, they rarely missed a bar mitzvah. To them, it was like Off-Off-Broadway.

And there I was, a "boy" three thousand impossible Hebrew words away from becoming a "man," in a dark itchy wool suit, which I was forced to change into on account of, shortly before leaving the house, a Cocker Spaniel named Blackie leaped up on my linen gray suit (a garment much better suited than wool for the steamy month of August) and got dog shit all over it. Completing the ensemble was a white satin *yarmulke* and a wool prayer shawl. Elvis Presley I was not.

I couldn't make heads or tails of those weird squiggly words. It was all Greek to me. Even worse, it was all Hebrew. So, I did what any "boy" in my predicament would've done: faked it.

I chanted and sang in a gibberish double-talk (a trick I picked up watching Sid Caesar schtick) and mimicked the sounds and cadences of this foreign Hebraic tongue. Not out of disrespect, mind you, but out of sheer panic. I did manage, however, to memorize the first line of my *maftir*, so it started off on the right foot: "Ah-nee-yo-ho, so-ah-rawl, low-oh-nu-chhhulmo—" But then every line, thereafter, became pure horseshit. Mumbo jumbo nonsense. And I sang this gibberish not like a cantor—no, like Sinatra!

At first, it appeared that the synagogue elders were in awe as they seesawed to the rhythm. My father's associates were impressed by my apparent expertise in the Scripture and give Dad sotted nods of approval.

But, then I glanced at the cantor, his face buried in his hands in shame. Oy. Then I locked eyes with my revered grandparents and saw Ben and Sarah's utter disappointment. Oy vey!

Well, at least my dad looked proud as spiked punch, winking at me, giving me the thumbs up, as if his kid just sank a half-court buzzer-beater. He never knew his son could fake it so well, and was positive his boy would grow up to become an even greater huckster than his dear ol' dad.

Finally, thankfully, I decided to hit the last gibberish note. Dad started to applaud but stopped when it was immediately apparent that he was the only one clapping.

"Mazel tov," the rabbi said, kindly—for he was a man who evidently had seen far worse tragedies.

"Hey, Sinatrastein," said one of the bearded Hasidic elders. "Mazel tov, my tuchis! Sonny boy, you just single-handedly set the Jews back five thousand years!"

And, well . . . having ceremoniously turned thirteen, I took it like a *man*.

* * *

1974

A CONDOM NAMED SMECKY

If Necessity is the mama of invention, who's the papa?

In my case, it was Comedy.

Not wishing to eke out an existence on a writer's stipends alone, I launched a little invention called the Pet Rubber.

It was along the lines of the Pet Rock, only more practical. The Pet Rubber was packaged in a miniature pet carrier. Even had "air holes"—the carrier, not the condom. It was promoted as "the first condom that's user-friendly." Inside each package, along with, of course, quality condoms, was a humorous (yet highly instructive) Care & Training Booklet. Because, let's face it, many a horny greenhorn knew not what they were doing. For example, you can't put a rubber on once you've unrolled it. Pretty simple, huh? Well, I didn't know that the "first time" I used one (or tried to) many moons

335

ago. And, no one—especially in the heat of the moment—ever stopped what he was doing to read a condom's detailed instructions. You carried the thing in your wallet—for years, maybe—till you got lucky. At least, that's what it was like way back when I was a teen.

Pet Rubbers sold like hotcakes. That's *if* hotcakes were made of latex and designed to slip over an erection. It was something an aunt—a cool one—might "gift" a nephew or niece. On the cover of the Care & Training Booklet was a playful cartoon of a topless woman saying to a bare-chested man, "Cute. What does it do besides play dead?"

Then, unfolded, the booklet read: "Say hello to your very own Pet Rubber. And kiss unsafe sex goodbye." It was not only instructive, but also entertaining. For instance, it suggested naming your Pet Rubber as you would a puppy. (I named mine Smecky.)

And teaching your Pet Rubber tricks. Like how to roll over. Or play dead. (Yes, this was years before the advent of Viagra and Cialis.)

The Pet Rubber helped eliminate the stigma of buying condoms. Which is why it became the first condom to be sold Point-Of-Sale, right there next to the register and chewing gum. The POS display sign read: "Adopt a Pet Rubber." It wasn't just available at pharmacies, either—you could get a Pet Rubber just about anywhere. 7-Elevens, Longs Drugs, novelty shops, beauty stores, and cosmetic counters.

With zero advertising dollars, its promotion had to be equally inventive. So, to get the word out, I deployed an old-school tactic. Or, should I say, Old Gold tactic. Back when television was in its infancy (and so was I), a particular TV commercial for Old Gold cigarettes fascinated me. A dancer costumed in a large, oversized replica of an Old Gold cigarette pack danced with a box of matches, its only visible human features were white-gloved bare arms and long, very shapely legs. (I was just a boy, but already a "leg man.") Right about the same time I came up with the idea for Pet Rubbers, I was hired by Steve Silver, the mastermind behind San Francisco's spectacular smash hit *Beach Blanket Babylon*, to write dialogue (mostly celebrity-related jokes and sight gags). Touted as "the longest-running musical comedy in the world," it showcased zany costumes and outrageously oversized hats. Val Diamond, one of its stars, wore upon her curly head the entire skyline of San Francisco. I kid you not. I'm talking Transamerica Pyramid, Golden Gate Bridge, Ferry Building Clock Tower, a Chinese Pagoda, and the dome of City Hall. If you're seated close to the stage, you might even spot my apartment. This remarkable hat was fourteen feet tall, nine feet wide and weighed more than two hundred and fifty pounds, but it didn't prevent Val from wowing the crowd as she belted out "San Francisco" like a combination Jeanette MacDonald-Ethel Merman.

I must admit, along with the dancing pack of Old Gold cigarettes, BBB was truly inspirational. An example of its showmanship and razzmatazz: someone would sing "Ebb Tide" (*First the tide rushes in—*) as a giant box of Tide detergent rushes in, shapely legs and all. Sure, they were sight gags, but eye-popping sight gags. So, I asked Steve where I might get a costume made of a giant-sized Pet Rubber package. The sweet man that he was, he hooked me up with Chris March, the mastermind costume designer.

And then came the night I discovered Miss Pet Rubber.

When I first spotted Michi in a nightclub called Oasis, she was working as a Peachy Puff Cigarette & Candy Girl wearing short shorts. One glance at those amazing "Betty Grable" legs and I offered her the job. Miss Pet Rubber went everywhere. Championship prizefights, Super Bowls, trade shows, college campuses, and, if she strolled past a construction site, oh my, how the hardhats would wolf-whistle!

Her luscious leggy image appeared in just about every newspaper and magazine. It was no small feat getting your product seen by so many without having to fork over the big bucks for advertising. All this "free" exposure helped promote safe sex and—because it came out at the peak of the AIDS epidemic—saved more than a few lives.

It also sold quite a few Pet Rubbers.

Looking back, it's safe to say Pet Rubbers made a great number of lovers grin, while also making them fucking safer. Literally.

I had some other inventive ideas. One of which was Throx, The Cure for The Missing Sock. I came up with the idea of packaging socks in threes after having lost one too many in the wash. Throx took off like a rocket, and was awarded "America's Best Innovation" by *Reader's Digest*, was featured on *The Today Show* with Kathie Lee and *The Big Idea* with Donnie Deutsch.

Oh, and, yes . . . Season One of *Shark Tank*.

Here's a little slice of life after Shark Tank:

"Say," says some stranger on the street, "aren't you . . . ? Yeaaah! You're him, alright! You're, uh, whatsisface! The three sock guy! Am I right? AM I RIGHT!? Fuckin' A, I'm right! HEY, EMMA—OVER HERE! Look! I got . . . I got . . . uh, what's your name, buddy?"

"Edwin Heaven."

"Yeah! Fuckin' Edward Haven. Right here, folks! Emma! Hurry! Bring the kids! Bring the camera! We got the three sock guy here!!"

But, hey—that's another story. (Hmm, I think I smell a sequel.)

throx.com · Photo: Victoria Smith

* * *

EDWIN HEAVEN

ACKNOWLEDGEMENTS

Thank you . . . Arthur Gilbert, for introducing me to the joy of reading. Buddy Gilbert, for introducing me to the joy of writing. Nan Gilbert, for being a joy to write for. Marcia Gilbert Nax, for lavishing affection and your delicious varnishkas and chopped liver. My grandparents Sarah and Ben, for being exactly that—*grand* parents. Audrey and Brendon, for giving me so much—especially three amazing grandchildren: Sully, Larkin and RiRi. And much love and puppy licks to my four-legged children, past and present: Tulip, Harley, Ben, Sally and King. (Oh how I wish a doggy's lifespan could be as long as a cockatoo's or a turtle's or George Burns'.)

And a whole lotta lovin' and thanks to . . . Marguerite Gaffney, Prairie Prince, Re Styles, Marshall Terrill, Barbi McQueen, Carmella Scaggs, Michael TD, Sandra Keller Palesch, Virginia MacGregor, Michael Lerner, Joy Nordenstrom, Jeff Trager, Devroux McKay, Heather Emelin Graham, Hollie Stevens, Phree Bartley, Pamela Courson, Renata Gonzales (and little Ari), Janet Margolin, Bobby Slayton, Gina Hurley, Mary Bond, Morgan Giulianelli, Brian Finley, Libby Staub, Dre Brewer, Heather O' Donovan, Denise Pazienti, Daisaku Ikeda, Gabriela Rivas, Laurie Nave, Andrew Kent, Robert Altman, Victoria Smith, Jonathan Postal, Rabbit Jones, Alejandro Escovedo, Nancy Rankin, Jennifer Miro and Jeff Olener. Oh, and let us not forget: David Bowie, Iggy Pop, Jimi Hendrix, Mick Jagger, Peter Green, John Madara, Lance Anderson, Ron Polte, Jerry Pompili, Joel Selvin, Herb Caen, Strange de Jim, Dirk Dirkson, Cynthia Bowman, Sally Mann Romano, Elizabeth "McSis" McKenzie, Christopher Moore, Laura Albert a.k.a. JT LeRoy, T.C. Boyle, Kurt "Daffodil-11" Vonnegut, Don Carpenter, Liz Hasse, Cherie Currie, Marie Currie, Patricia Crane, Jerry Gibbons, Bobby Pritikin, Jon Hyde, Jim and Betty Emison, Julietta Hay, Donna Gorman, Lou Grimaldi, Sandi Gilbert, Lenny Kauffman, Maury Kelisky, Glenn Cooney, Dean Freedlander, Francis Coppola, Joe Sedelmaier, Chris Brown, Ron Turner, Peter Shanaberg, Reenie and Millie McDonnell, Tony Gemignani, Jesus Alvarez, Steve Lynch, Rich and Laura Azzolino, Kathy Petrucci, Sarah Royer, Sam Askin, The Chimps, SFOG (Fredo, Barry, Eyad), WB Coyle, Wayne Whelan, Cannibal Carl, Johnny Bocchetti, Angie Seegers, Kari Zanotto, Tommy Rickard, Elizabeth Austin, Frank Lauria, Ellen Smith, Jim English, Sandi Harrington, Laurie and Vince Welnick, Rick Anderson, Nicolette Dalpino, Tish Kronen-Gluck, Shanda Lorenz, Rosita Brandis, Liz Hasse, Margaret Person, Heather Moore, Bob Tully, Michael Duffy, Tom Freyer, Mary Bonn, Sabrina Bodnar, Summer Givens, Lina Elliliä, Carissa Villafaña, and Takara Noel (wherever you are).

And last but certainly not least, thank you everyone who, in one way or another, helped carry me across the finish line.

"A sweet, shameless wisecracking wonder of a book. . . a little bit West, a little bit Toole, a little bit Robbins—the rest is pure Heaven!"

—JOHN HAWKES

Academy Award Nominee actor, *Winters Bone, Deadwood, Sessions*

"Look out world, Edwin Heaven is the next big thing in modern-day literature. He's every superlative I can think of: funny, intelligent, twisted, perverted. The World's Most Handsome Man is from the mind of a demented genius."

—MARSHAL TERRILL

Author of Steve McQueen: *Portrait of an American Rebel*

"Edwin Heaven writes like hell!"

—SAN FRANCISCO CHRONICLE

"Wayne Grant is destined to become one of the great literary heroes of all time. Kind of like Mr. Darcy, but not as smoldering, Rhett Butler, but not as sexy, Captain Von Trapp but with a much bigger ass. Mr. Grant bumbled and blundered his way into the frigid and forgotten chambers of my bitter heart. I laughed, I cried–this book became a part of me."

—LAUREL MAY

Editor, 944 *Magazine*

www.ingramcontent.com/pod-product-compliance
Lightning Source LLC
Chambersburg PA
CBHW071707120626
46550CB00001B/137

* 9 7 9 8 2 1 8 4 1 6 2 1 8 *